TRAINING FOR THE THEATRE

Premises & Promises

MICHEL SAINT-DENIS

edited by
Suria Saint-Denis

THEATRE ARTS BOOKS
NEW YORK

HEINEMANN
LONDON

Published in the United States by
THEATRE ARTS BOOKS
153 Waverly Place
New York, N.Y. 10014

ISBN-0-87830-576-9 (Paperbound)
Library of Congress Catalog No. 81-86083

Published in Great Britain by
HEINEMANN EDUCATIONAL BOOKS LTD.
22 Bedford Square
London WC1B 3HH

ISBN-0-435-18795-3

Designed by Bernard Schleifer

Manufactured in the United States of America

Passages from *My Life in Art* by Constantin Stanislavski and from *Theatre: The Rediscovery of Style* by Michel Saint-Denis are used with the permission of the publisher, Theatre Arts Books, 153 Waverly Place, New York, N.Y. 10014. *My Life in Art:* Copyright, 1924, by Little, Brown, and Company. Copyright, 1948, Elizabeth Reynolds Hapgood. Copyright renewed 1952. *Theatre: The Rediscovery of Style:* © 1960 by Michel Saint-Denis.

The quotation from Antonin Artaud's *Oeuvres Completes, Volume 4: The Theatre and Its Double,* pp. 85 and 87, is used by permission of Editions Gallimard, 5 Rue Sebastien-Bottin 75341 Paris, John Calder (Publishers), Ltd., London, and Grove Press, Inc., New York. © 1964 Editions Gallimard. Copyright © 1958 by Grove Press, Inc. The excerpt from Georges Charbonnier's *Essai sur Antonin Artaud,* p. 180, is used with the permission of Editions Robert Laffont, 6, Place Saint-Sulpice, 75279 Paris. The excerpt from T. S. Eliot's *Poetry and Drama* (Cambridge: Harvard University Press, 1951) is used with the permission of Harvard University Press. The excerpt from *The New York Herald-Tribune,* January 18, 1959, is used with the permission of Walter Kerr.

Epigraphs in this book, where not attributed to others, are by Michel Saint-Denis.

For Suria

ACKNOWLEDGMENTS

MY DEEP-FELT GRATITUDE goes to George Zournas, editor and publisher of Theatre Arts Books, for giving me so generously of his time and invaluable advice, for having shared with me this journey through Michel Saint-Denis' life and writings, for laughing with me through difficult moments, for never failing to encourage me. Without him this book would never have seen the light of day.

I also want to express my heartfelt thanks to Stephen Aaron, Michel's and my loyal friend, for his devotion and assistance in preparing the material for this book.

I am grateful to my dear friend Robert Chapman of Harvard University, who was the first to translate my husband's American lectures, to John D. Rockefeller III, who was instrumental in bringing us to America in 1958, and to William Schuman and Mark Schubart, who were President and Dean of the new Juilliard School.

My very special thanks are extended to the Ford Foundation and W. McNeil Lowry, its Vice President. Mr. Lowry, at the suggestion of Rosamond Gilder, John Houseman, Dr. Peter Mennin and Robert M. MacGregor, obtained a grant from the Ford Foundation which allowed us to work uninterruptedly on the preparation of this book.

To the Motleys—Sophie Devine, Margaret Harris and Elizabeth Montgomery—for their continuing friendship over the years and for their permitting me to reproduce the Motley skirt design in this book, I am most grateful.

My thanks are addressed to the many friends who organised our archives in London: to Annette Brinkworth, to Sandy Black, to Nicholas Mackenzie and, last but not least, to Norman Sims, the Custodian of the Saint-Denis Archives.

I acknowledge with pleasure my indebtedness to Marian Seldes, who read various versions of the manuscript and gave considerate and knowledgeable advice, and to Elaine Hallett, who, with great patience and understanding, helped me to finish the editing.

My thanks are also offered to those who provided me—the eternal traveller—with surroundings which proved most congenial for writing: Rosamond Gilder in New York, Jocelyn Herbert in London, Zoe Caldwell and Robert Whitehead in Connecticut, and friends, too numerous to name, in Montreal.

SURIA SAINT-DENIS

CONTENTS

LIST OF ILLUSTRATIONS

TRAINING FOR THE THEATRE

Suria and Michel Saint-Denis

INTRODUCTION

THIS BOOK WAS PLANNED and written by my husband, Michel Saint-Denis, as a guide for the teaching of theatre; it is meant for actors, directors, technicians—all those who guide acting students in their first steps towards acquiring the tools of their craft. It is not basically an exposition of new concepts but is intended to show ways of encouraging organic growth and to provide a framework for that growth. It is based on his experience as an actor, director, teacher and lecturer.

Michel Saint-Denis had the good fortune to be born in an era of great change. Over the course of fifty years, as his work and life took him to many countries, he was a witness to the manifold "isms" of his times: naturalism, realism, expressionism, symbolism and many others. All this contributed to his development.

When he started teaching, he had gone through long periods of research, but he had no doctrines or pre-established methods which he followed; it was clear to him that, in time and with experience, these would take form. For him, to begin with, all was invention, discovery and liberty, with liberty's inseparable complement, *discipline*—the discipline that produces techniques which free the actor and establish him in the skills of his craft.

To him, a school was not only a place to learn from the past; he felt it should also be a place to try out new ideas and to experiment in ways not possible in the commercial theatre. His fundamental aim was to provide in each school a comprehensive framework of techniques around which the students' initiative, imagination and invention could be developed. He offered the students a remarkable vision—but he also gave them the tools to achieve that vision.

Michel worked on this book, off and on, for the last ten years of his life. It is based on a carefully prepared plan he left which sets out in great detail the specific material he wanted to use and the way in which he planned to use it. Most of the work had been done when he died. After Michel's death, Robert M. MacGregor and George Zournas, the publishers of Theatre Arts Books—which had brought out Michel's earlier book, *Theatre: The Rediscovery of Style*—encouraged me to complete the organisation of that great mass of material and edit it for publication.

Much of the written material was in French, as were the conversations between the two of us which we had recorded on tapes over the years to help refresh his memory. The obstacles to translating this material often seemed insurmountable. How could one, without betraying the original, translate such a unique and very personal idiom from one language to another? Because this extraordinary idiom developed out of Michel's need to evoke effectively those images he conjured up to demonstrate his points—I was determined to match Michel's own way of expression as closely as possible.

In one of his letters to a friend, I found the following passage: "Everything, as you know, depends on the doing, on how things are *understood* and *done*. How is one to make this concrete? I meet this difficulty constantly in trying to write my book."

In another note he said: "I am working to the limit of my strength—with anger and modesty."

Though he knew how to use his knowledge with unusual insight and though he possessed a remarkable foresight, Michel was open to criticism and never feared being proved wrong. He was used, misunderstood and, sometimes, hated, but he was also accepted, admired and loved. Questioning himself constantly about his ideas, analysing his achievements, risking mistakes, he often ventured into the unknown. That is what made working with him a rich challenge, renewed every hour, and living with him an act of total commitment.

SURIA SAINT-DENIS

London - Montreal - New York

FOREWORD

MICHEL SAINT-DENIS' LIFE was a quest for truth in the theatre. In this book, you will find the patterns of his life as they reflect this quest, not as high principles but as sometimes contradictory responses to different circumstances. For Michel, his own contradictions were signs of his own renewal and continuing growth.

Who was this man really? An intellectual who was instinctive; a "paysan" who was an aristocrat; a radical who was careful to conserve the past; a man of control who fought recklessly for his beliefs; sceptical and responsible; ironic and dedicated—I can hear Michel laugh at my inability to categorise him.

He was a Frenchman whose influence on British theatre has directly touched and changed all of us over the age of thirty-five and indirectly the generations to come. Four major theatres—the Royal Court, the National Theatre, the English National Opera and the Royal Shakespeare Company—all owe part of their way of working to him.

Remembering the man of the theatre, I also remember the man who in the war years turned to what was then more important than the theatre. He was head of the French Section of the BBC and, as the legendary Jacques Duchesne, spoke almost every evening to his countrymen in the name of Free France with that combination of perception, civilization and sense of the value of human communication which, they will still tell you in France, gave courage, hope and human dignity.

My own personal debt to Michel is enormous. In 1961, at my request, he joined the directors of the Royal Shakespeare Company. It was young, messy, bustling, adventurous—all over the place—and he, a man of great wisdom, decided to join the adventure. I was a very lucky young man. He gave me ballast and direction when it was critically needed.

Perhaps English pragmatism, our "openness"—a favorite word of Michel's—attracted him to us. Our "openness" also made us love to remain amateurs, using dislike of theory as an excuse for avoiding craft, a danger of which Michel never failed to remind us. What he did for the Royal Shakespeare Company and for me, its young director, is quite incalculable. He spoke to a new generation of young actors about the European heritage, about Stanislavski, Copeau, Brecht. He had known these men and worked with them. But he did not give us cold theory. Michel hated dogma. He knew well how quickly yesterday's truth becomes today's comfortable convention, imitated unthinkingly and without effect.

He was a superb teacher who loved the young. For him, the young were instinctive and giving: he took from them as much as he gave. They were also dogmatic and obstinate; but not for long with Michel. And theory was always subjected to his sceptical (and very Gallic!) challenge. He believed, of course, in craft, in technique, but only as *means*. Acting was not a trick to be learned and then performed; it was not imitation, but rather revelation of the whole human personality. He had a deep-rooted suspicion of any "method"—old or new—of anything which stopped questions or inhibited change. *His* method was challenge and change.

It was from these years with Michel that I began to understand the responsibility of the theatre. If you invite an audience to surrender two or three hours of their lives to you, you must offer something considerable in return. It is better to fail than to repeat an empty pattern.

Michel felt that all of us in the theatre are responsible in our work not just for displaying our talents to their best advantage, but also for being at our best as people. For him, the two qualities were one, indistinguishable. Talent did not excuse unbalanced or selfish behaviour: talent was only diminished by it.

His favorite question about a colleague with whom he was about to work was: "Is he in a good state?" If he was in a good state he would do good work. If not, then he should be persuaded to have a holiday or a rest. He ought not risk wasting the time of the theatre or the theatre's audience. Michel was very careful of people.

When I think of Michel, I think also of Suria, his wife. They were inseparable—collaborators (and arguers) in everything. So this preface is a tribute to her also; for her work, for editing this book, and for her dedication in handing on what I believe to be a great tradition to a new generation at the Juilliard School in New York.

The reasons why any of us work in the theatre are complex. Many use it like the childhood nursery—an easy place to enter the world of fantasy, to hide. For Michel, the theatre was not a place to hide: it was a place to *be*. Its purpose is to reveal the man.

Michel Saint-Denis was a great man. Because of this he was a great man of the theatre. His work was based on cherishing the quality of the human being. His career is a testament to his own quality, his own integrity. He was the sworn enemy of dead convention. For Michel, the truth was something which changes as our lives change; the search for truth, never-ending. It is not a comfortable conclusion, but it is alive.

PETER HALL

London

AFTERWORD

MICHEL SAINT-DENIS' IRREPLACEABLE book is meant to prepare serious aspirant actors for an institutional theatre whose repertory
would consist of the great dramatic literature of the past and the
progressive drama of the present; such institutional theatre is
represented at its best in Great Britain, France and Austria, where
traditions of patronage initiated by princes continue today justified as social and cultural necessities. Unfortunately, theatre as
an independent institutional entity is rare in the United States
and nowhere enjoys the permanent state support—national or
metropolitan—which has long been a feature of European culture.
In the United States, to be sure, we are blessed with regional
theatres, but their companies are recruited from players, however
capable, without a common schooling, tradition or style. They
are assembled by accident, and can count on but little uninter-
rupted work, to say nothing of permanent tenure, and commercial
competition constantly threatens the top ranks of any really good
regional group.

There are very few places in America where a serious student
can learn—and practice—how to enact an *other*, a person or character composed of elements of behaviour apart from the habits
of the student's own unformed and quite accidentally acquired
"personality." What we have instead are numerous "schools,"
most of them mere studios which actually provide only elementary formulae enabling ambitious young aspirants, with or with-

out talent, to manipulate their given personalities in ways that will make them lucrative to agents who will somehow find them jobs in TV soap-operas, in films or, sometimes, in the commercial theatre.

In the current American sense, "personality" is by no means that individual selfhood which can be suspended from the basic ego and projected imaginatively beyond and against the actor's essential self. The "personality" offered to the film industry and the commercial theatre is nothing more than a bundle of characteristics accumulated around the core of energy of an undeveloped post-adolescent. Grace of person, physical attractiveness and superficial charm are often quite enough to launch spectacular—albeit brief—careers with nothing more than the help of a canny director who knows how to exploit such idiosyncratic potential. Usually this so-called "personality" is straitjacketed into narcissistic exhibitionism, into simulacra of natural behaviour, which can be effective for a time if it meets the limited needs of our dramatic journalism. But when their energy and talent are exhausted, these "personalities" are quickly and easily replaced by others of the same sort.

It is not easy for young people to find their true centre, but the half-dozen schools which Saint-Denis inaugurated provided a concrete foundation for those young men and women who had the philosophical fortitude, the energy and patience, to equip themselves for the difficult mystery of playing an *other* rather than their own given selves. It was not that their individuality was diminished; rather, they were given means to develop and expand that individuality beyond their habits of preference and indulgence. With Saint-Denis, instead of accepting the routine conditioning of the everyday, the unfledged performers were led into the possibility of polymorphous projection. This book presumes a *tabula rasa* which, by the multiform exercises presented here, can be turned into a transparent mirror reflecting the vast diversity of human behaviour. This training is rigourous, exhausting as well as exhaustive, but the result, the aim of all Saint-Denis' labours, is the creation of a completely equipped stage performer who can turn mind and body into any and all otherness. This is not to claim that the plans here proposed are the only ones that might be useful to a student. However, laid beside other proposals, they may be judged by their authority, their scope and their efficiency in leading acting students towards that ultimate goal. It is indeed, only a single path, but it is the path which the greatest contemporary actors of Britain and France have put to compelling use. The roster of those who, in one way or another, have collaborated with or have been influenced by Michel Saint-Denis is testimony enough to show how well his way has worked.

The mere fact that a plan of practical possibilities is offered here by no means suggests that such possibilities are easily achieved. Suffering is always part of the process, and patronage, whether from public or private pockets, is more often than not intermittent, whimsical and inadequate. The records of Saint-Denis' own companies—their births as small seedlings, their growth, blossoming and dispersal—are clinical descriptions of the economic and metaphysical limitations of the times in which those companies existed. Few are prepared to accept the great artistic responsibilities and the poverty of material reward that is the destiny of those involved in such endeavours. But fortunately there are selfless martyrs of theatre, just as there are martyrs of music and painting. That Saint-Denis brought to fruition such a vast harvest despite two world wars, economic catastrophe and "normal" indifference is a heartening sign to others that persistence, plus talent and intelligence, can win.

Even assuming they are willing to invest years in learning their craft, one must ask, as many young actors do not, where, except occasionally in subsidiary positions and on a very tentative basis, will they eventually be able to practice that craft? It is a question that should also be posed by aspiring musicians, singers and dancers. It is unfortunately the case that even our most eminent schools are often irresponsible, in that they permit beginners to assume that the mere possession of ambition and a trace of aptitude will equip them for triumphs. Energy, stubborness, faith and hope are by no means reliable partners; not everyone can do everything. Much heartbreak could be avoided if overly permissive parents and their stage-struck children would read this book and then decide if the young person has the temperament to face the real situation vis-à-vis the current economy and his or her true capacities. Then the work analysed and programmed in the pages of this book could be a true rod and staff. But such clear-eyed people are rare; those who exist must look across the Atlantic for evidence of the value of so demanding an apprenticeship.

Whatever the decline of the British empire in its political seignory, whatever tensions and pressures exist in the United Kingdom, one fact is supremely evident: theatre in England today is of an expressive and operational quality which leads the world. The past and present programme of the National Theatre, with its repertory encompassing the traditional and the contemporary, has been and is supported to the last seat by the public and by generous tax funds. The Royal Shakespeare Company provides dazzling productions, one after another, with a company of virtuoso performers second to none. The innovations of the Royal Court continue the great tradition of Vedrenne and Granville-Barker, George Devine and John Osborne. Regional theatre, with civic and national support, continues to produce new generations of accomplished professionals. The lyric imagination of the English language is continuously revived in theatres all over the island.

This has been made abundantly clear to Americans over the last quarter century: anything of genuine distinction which Broadway has shown, to a very great degree, has been born in the theatres in London; American television has been, in large part, salvaged by British television spectaculars.

What was perhaps the greatest theatrical experience since the end of the Second World War was the presentation on Broadway in 1981 of *Nicholas Nickleby* by the Royal Shakespeare Company. The last instance of such explosive grandeur on Broadway was the 1950 season of the Old Vic Company, which included the unforgettable repertory of *Henry IV, Uncle Vanya* and—directed by Michel Saint-Denis—*Oedipus Rex* with Laurence Olivier. Then Saint-Denis was alive and present with proofs of his labors brilliantly manifest. In *Nicholas Nickleby*, although conceived without his presence, there was observed, nevertheless, the *eminence grise* of his mind and practice. So much of the quality in its kaleidoscopic eight hours of acrobatic tumult and heart-breaking drama, in its complex cohesion of mimicry and spoken words, came from an elite corps of thoroughly trained professionals, wholly absorbed in the multiplicity, the other-ness, of their shifting roles. Using techniques of suggestion which Saint-Denis' methods of improvisatory action make possible, those actors showed us coaches fully loaded, city streets crammed, theatres in mad performance, the stews and horrors of Dickens' tragedy, all with the simplest means and most electrifying effect. The intensity of the play's heroic figures was truly Shakespearian: the personifications of Nicholas himself, his terrible uncle, the horrible Squeers, and, above all, the protean impersonation of the wounded, ravaged Smike, established a criterion of performance which will last a long time. The mercurial brilliance, speed and surprise of their continual transformation, personage upon personage, depended on attitudes and skills which the training of Saint-Denis achieves, aided and abetted through the work of his companions, George Devine, Glen Byam Shaw and Trevor Nunn. Here was invention we had thought to exist only in the grandest lyric concepts incarnate in a fellowship of artists which made the most difficult-to-achieve potentials actually present in the flesh.

If and when such an institutional theatre with a body of sub-ventioned actors is realized in this country, the complete design for the preparation of its actors and for the organization of its activity is available—analysed and programmed in these pages by Michel Saint-Denis and his wife Suria, with the collaboration and support of those whose names appear in this book.

LINCOLN KIRSTEIN

New York
January 1, 1982

PART ONE

Jacques Copeau

Chapter One

PREMISES AND PROMISES

Premises

IT WAS ANDRÉ GIDE who said "Jacques Copeau has inscribed his name deeply in the history of the theatre; the French stage is no longer the same since his glorious efforts at the Théâtre du Vieux Colombier." I was proud that he was my uncle—my mother's brother. It was he who, after my father's early death, began to take care of our family.

I was attracted to him as if to a magnet and it was he who inexorably drew my whole life towards the theatre, *his* theatre—the Vieux Colombier. As a boy I played truant to go and see him rehearse during the day, and then in the evening would go back to the theatre again to watch him act. When, after the end of the first World War, I returned to France from the Far East, there was no question in my mind: I had to join him in his work. I was twenty-two.

During the next ten years as an apprentice, collaborator and close friend of Copeau, I learned my craft. It was he who revealed the theatre to me and led me to discoveries that were to illuminate my way for many years to come.

I joined him in 1920 and for the next four years all my days and evenings were spent at the Théâtre du Vieux Colombier. In addition to helping Copeau with the general planning, I undertook part of the stage management and administrative responsibilities, such as working in public relations and in the box office.

From time to time I acted in the plays and I also made regular
visits to Copeau's school in order to follow the training of a small
group of actors of my own age. Their exercises, experimental in
nature, excited my curiosity.

In 1924, exhausted by years of planning and anxiety over finances, Copeau decided to leave Paris. With his family, some
members of his company and a small group of student actors, he
settled in Burgundy, in a village near Beaune—Pernand-Verge-
lesse. There he pursued his work in an old *cuverie*, a converted
barn. I was now a regular member of the company and it was
there that we went on to experiment with various ways of improvisation, later adding comic and character improvisations with
and without masks.

Over the course of five years we built up a large audience in
the towns and villages around Beaune. Many in our audiences
had never been to a theatre. They liked our repertory and our
way of acting, which was mostly improvisational and which was
generally more to be *seen* than *heard*. Our comic improvisations
were instantly accepted by this audience. Because there was never
a barrier between players and audiences, the spectators sensed
how much they influenced the actors, how they could affect their
performances, indeed, how at times they could lift the actors to
a rare degree of exhilaration.

These shows had a kind of special fascination for our audiences
because we were using in our plays themes they could recognize.
For instance, soon after the wine harvest was over we performed
before two thousand vineyard workers, in the village of Nuits
Saint-Georges, a show which was based on their labour.

In another show we planned to have a group of shepherds,
ranged in a circle, who would enact in mime, dance, words and
song the story of the creation of the world. The circle would open
and close, move towards the audience and away from it. From
time to time the shepherds would form a long serpentine line
with the audience following them and then close into a circle
again.

Towards the end of the Burgundy period (1924-1929) we were
beginning to possess a more complete mode of expression, one
rich in possibilities; we could act, dance, sing, improvise in all
kinds of ways, and, when necessary, write our own dialogue. We

were then ready to devise shows that used these special techniques.

After our years with Copeau, we had, as he had foreseen, become an ensemble with a fertile imagination and the technical means to represent in our work many aspects and facets of the world. What we were lacking was, no doubt, a few more actors and, above all, a writer. Copeau understood that a basic condition for our success in producing that "oeuvre nouvelle," which he thought essential, was the discovery of the right kind of author, a kind of reincarnation of Aeschylus or Shakespeare, someone, perhaps, like Lorca.

In 1929 Copeau decided to stop all work in Burgundy and encouraged us to return to Paris. He was already more ill than he himself realized; we were quite unaware of the seriousness of his condition.

In Paris Copeau introduced us to a talented young dramatist, André Obey. Then, reassured, he went his independent way and returned to Burgundy and I started my own company. The marvelous adventure of the Vieux Colombier with Copeau had ended.

Copeau had begotten us; it was, no doubt, unseemly to expect him to beget *for* us.

The recollection of the Théâtre du Vieux Colombier that comes first to my mind is of the stage itself: it was both wide and high and every part of it was open to the auditorium. A forestage—on the same level as the main stage—projected into the auditorium to form another acting area, easily recognizable as such. It was designed for *physical* acting; its form, its many levels, its steps and aprons, allowed for a great variety of staging. The whole stage was an acting area, in contrast to that "box of illusions"—the proscenium stage. It gave an equal authenticity to classical farce, poetic drama and realistic "anti-theatrical" plays. It rejected any kind of painted or visual illusion, any kind of naturalistic decor created by sets and complicated lighting. Stage screws could get no footing in its cement floor.

The tyranny of stage-hands and electricians, with their complex techniques of set changing, had been eliminated, to the great advantage of the plays and the actors. We were able to put on seven different plays each week as it was easy to change the decor between matinee and evening performances. And as the technicians no longer had the upper hand, the stage was often free for rehearsals. In a repertory theatre, as the Vieux Colombier was, it is of great importance that directing and acting be developed in the very space where the plays will "live" for the audience, that is, on the stage rather than in a rehearsal room.

As I remember that stage, precise images of the plays I saw on it come to my mind—images that left a deep impression on me. It is not so much the emotional impact of these plays that remain in my memory as their visual aspects—differences in style which marked each production with a well-defined physical form. To me each play seemed to leave traces of its pattern on the stage-floor, each design unique, different from every other. I remember actors in characteristic positions and attitudes. I see not only individuals, but groups of actors, scenes in motion, sequences which revive in me—no doubt clarified and heightened by time—the memory of those first revelations.

That bare stage and the way it was equipped did away with naturalistic illusion. The actor was not exhibited as if in a pictorial composition, as if he were part of a painting—he did not merge into the atmosphere to the point of disappearance. He was as if poised for action, isolated, thrown into relief, detached in a free, three-dimensional space. He was like a puppet, constantly animated from within yet magnetized by the audience and the surrounding air, his body and voice translating physically the poetic contents of the play.

To illustrate physical differences in style, I would like to use as examples some of Copeau's productions: *Les Fourberies de Scapin* by Molière and *Le Pacquebot S.S. Tenacity* by Charles Vildrac, both done in 1920, and *Twelfth Night* by Shakespeare, which Copeau first directed in 1914.

For *Scapin*, Copeau had a bare wooden platform constructed with steps descending from it, which was set in the centre of the permanent cement stage—quite isolated. It was lit by a large triangle of lights hung above it, which flooded the surface with a white, harsh brilliance.

The actors played both on the platform and around it. The younger actors could leap up onto the platform with an exuberant wildness, while the older characters were obliged to climb the steps laboriously.

The platform, with its uneven wooden surface, was hollow, and therefore resonant and springy. This intensified, in a pleasant manner, the sounds made on it, either by the stamping, jumping feet of the younger characters or by the slow stomping of their elders accompanied by the tapping of walking sticks. In the swiftly moving scenes of pursuit, the actors, leaping from the hard coldness of the cement floor up onto the warm, resounding wooden platform and back down again, created a kind of by-play of sound.

There was a perfect integration between the characterization of the different roles, the "physical" acting, and the acting space. Out of this theatrical "enlargement" flashed both the lyricism of farce and the poetry of comedy; human nature revealed itself in all its complexity, its generosity as well as its implacability.

For his setting of Shakespeare's *Twelfth Night,* Copeau used a grand staircase, a plain white semi-circular bench and a few shrubs. These neutral indications allowed the actors to transform the acting areas through Shakespeare's poetry, as the characters led us from sea-shore to palace or garden. The many different scenes followed one another without blackout or any changes of decor—never slow, never heavy—and thus Shakespearian continuity was miraculously achieved.

The staging of *Scapin* was precise and specific: it was angular, jerky, violent and passionate—it seemed to leave traces of straight lines on the stage floor.

The Vieux Colombier's staging of *Twelfth Night,* on the contrary, "drew" curved lines; it was fluid, free, as if improvised. The comedians seemed to be inflated by air, or as if stuffed with straw—creatures of the imagination; they had neither the hair, hats, nor swords of ordinary historical reality, and their acting had a peculiar floating lightness.

When Copeau staged *Le Pacquebot S.S. Tenacity* by Charles Vildrac in 1920 he used the whole stage without any set—no material boundaries stopped the imagination from creating the intimacy of a seamen's cafe in a small seaport. A few chairs and tables, glasses and bottles were sufficient indications. There were no footlights, no proscenium and so no "fourth wall." All around—emptiness and shadows.

It was an extraordinary acting space. Copeau had achieved what he had foreseen in his famous Manifesto of 1913: "Pour l'oeuvre nouvelle, qu'on nous laisse un treteau nu." ("For the new work, give us an empty stage.")

But would not the cement stage floor and the emptiness overwhelm the poetic realism of the play? On the contrary, Antoine, the "Father of French Naturalism," an actor, director and drama critic, wrote of *Le Pacquebot S.S. Tenacity:* "The atmosphere is created with an almost unbearable intensity . . . Never before has such a complete *elimination* of theatrical elements been achieved. This demands a detailed perfection in acting. Never before have we attained such a degree of reality."

It seemed therefore that realism *had* been well served; or, better still, the bareness of the stage had intensified it. There was no "lying;" theatrical truth, the *physical* truth of the theatre, was thus represented in accord with the psychological truth of life. Although knowing we were at the theatre, we had no impression of being there: artifice had been eliminated. It was, as Mallarmé had written in another context long ago: "An empty stage at the service of invention."

All the plays at the Vieux Colombier were directed by Copeau himself and most of the time I was his stage-manager and rehearsal assistant. His actors would rehearse sotto voce, without any eloquence, careful not to force the text, just sketching tempo and rhythm without trying to achieve anything too early. During rehearsals Copeau would move ceaselessly from auditorium to the stage; if an actor was in difficulty he would talk to him freely but confidentially at the back of the stage.

An actor himself, he instinctively knew when to grant freedom to an actor and when to apply the right kind of pressure during the successive phases of rehearsals.

One of the outstanding actors in the Company, one whose way of rehearsing taught me most at that time, was Louis Jouvet. He worked lightly on his text, giving just enough voice to be heard by his fellow-players. He sketched his movements without setting them too early, concentrating on the relationship between his text and his moves, his walk, gestures, voice and moods. By remaining non-committed, he kept his spontaneity. Then, gradually, as this or that passage became clear, Jouvet would give it more voice and power but without stopping his self-observation.

Only towards the end of the rehearsals, when all relationships had fallen into place and had become familiar, did Jouvet begin to *act* his part. He had thought about it ceaselessly, but he never tried to *show* it before he was ready to *do* it; he never forced anything, and his "composition," always original, grew and flowered in a natural way.

Although I was present at all the rehearsals, I sometimes did not recognize Jouvet in his character when he appeared for the first time at the final dress rehearsal. His transformation did not come from costume or his make-up, which was always lightly indicated, but was brought into play by his subconscious—liberated, nourished, controlled.

In addition to Jouvet there were four or five actors with whom Copeau worked with great pleasure, but he worried about several others who were always falling into the same patterns.

When, after rehearsals, I went back with him to his office, he would sink into his armchair and doze for a few minutes—then waken and say to me: "Did you see them again today? I always know in advance what they are going to do. They cannot get out of themselves; they love only themselves. They reduce everything to the level of their own habits, their clichés, their affectations. They do not invent anything. It is all sheer imitation of imitation."

This problem of actors' limitations became a crucial one for Copeau. He became more and more aware of the contradiction between the freedom the bare stage could give and the encumbrances of his actors, hindered as they were by the dead traditions and false approaches which stemmed from the Romantic period and the bourgeois naturalistic theatre.

Copeau realised that the essence of theatre is not literary, but ritualistic and physical. He wanted to return to the sources, to primitive theatre, following through this the trend of the other arts of that period. There had been a temporary break between the disoriented artist-creator and the bewildered interpreter. Copeau felt that it was necessary to accept that break and to begin again. He envisioned a kind of laboratory attached to a theatre, but outside it, where, gradually a new kind of actor, an instrument of a new revitalized dramaturgy, could be evolved.

In 1920 Copeau established such a laboratory. He was adventuring into virgin territory in a fresh attempt to re-discover the secrets and the essence of acting.

He knew that acting, in order to be authentic, must be rooted in the very depth of self, but he also believed that the actor's inventiveness, in order to be liberated, needed a technique of physical and vocal expression. It could then flower in the interchange of ensemble acting.

Contemporary actors, in 1920, accustomed as they were to the conventions of naturalistic plays and the rigors and formality of the classics, either deflated the texts, taking no account of the quality, form and reality of their true style, or elaborated the texts so as to adorn themselves with words, to show off the beauty of the text as well as their own virtuosity, preening and strutting about like peacocks, but in borrowed plumage. Generally speaking, truth was distorted and dramatic authenticity was lost as well. Of course the texts sounded false; as for style, it had lost its power of direct revelation, and survived detached from meaning—artificial and boring.

Therefore in his teaching Copeau temporarily withdrew the use of texts and made the study of the expressiveness of the body—Improvisation—his point of departure. He led all the work in an empiric fashion, guided by experience, observation and experiment. With the support of his collaborators in various fields, he invented exercises with many progressions and developments.

He was very careful in choosing those who were allowed to attend his School/Laboratory. He believed that whether or not a student could become a genuine actor depended intimately on the nature of the student's character and the richness of his temperament. These two qualities he thought basic to an aspiring actor.

> In the history of the French theatre there are two periods: before and after Copeau.
>
> ALBERT CAMUS

Copeau had been at the center of questions that agitated many of his contemporaries in the world of the theatre: Craig, Appia,

Reinhardt, Stanislavski, and his followers, Meyerhold, Vachtan-
gov, and Tairov. Copeau had in his research gone much further
even than Meyerhold.

For example, Copeau, to enrich their studies, proposed that
his young actors work on a Japanese Nō—a form of theatre almost
completely unknown to the western world of that time. For this
work he chose the Nō play *Kantan*, using Arthur Waley's translation as its base. *Kantan* was done, not in order to reconstitute
a Nō, but to permit us to experience, to some degree, its ceremonial nature—a nature that seems beyond time. The Nō's convention is a free one: the actor announces to the audience who
he is and what he will do. There is a formal text, poetic and
rhythmical, often sung with subtly mimed movement. These
modes of expression organise themselves around the sounds issuing from a chorus supported by the pulsation of percussion
instruments. And, sometimes, when the drama needs to make
a point, the sound of a shrill piercing flute cuts through the beat
of the percussion.

Our performance of *Kantan*, which left the impression of a
spirited dream, was for me the incomparable summit of our work
in Copeau's School/Laboratory.

By his work, Copeau had altered the orientation of the theatre
in France. He had succeeded in renewing and transforming the
architecture of the stage, stage design, directing and acting.

One of the immediate artistic descendants of Jacques Copeau's
creative spirit was the Compagnie des Quinze (1929-1934) which
was the successor to the Burgundy group, Les Copiaux, reinforced
by a few more actors. I became its director—my first directorship.

The story of the Compagnie des Quinze concerns an excep-
tional experience: that of a creative theatre ensemble, devoted to
physical expression, which came to feel the need of an author.
With us, casting, staging and planning the sets and costumes
were undertaken at the same time as the writing of a play. It was
essential that the author become a member of our ensemble and
adhere to its orientation.

In André Obey, the writer whom Jacques Copeau introduced to us, we found such a person. So we began to work.

Over a period of time we worked on several themes. One of them was *The Battle of the Marne*, a famous incident of the 1914-1918 war.

We decided that we did not want to treat the subject as a series of anecdotes in a descriptive way; rather, we wanted to get to the roots of the event by a physical representation.

To give an idea of the epic dimensions which such a presentation can attain, here is a description of the process of the work:

Having decided on a tentative order of events, we improvised various scenes showing different aspects of everyday life in a village in peacetime. These scenes were done simultaneously.

Suddenly the bells of the church began to toll an alarm, warning that war had been declared. The inhabitants assembled in the village square. The moment of separation had arrived: the men called to the front and the distressed women left behind in the village. This was followed by the exodus of whole populations fleeing in panic before the invading Germans.

Scenes were improvised of men in combat, of life and work in the village, the anguish of women left behind. Finally, the armistice with its reunion of families and their realization of death and loss. Through our improvisations ideas gradually came to life and the framework of the play became clear.

Obey made use of our previous experiments, in which we acted several scenes simultaneously. He evolved a mode of expression, a kind of "musical" composition which used some real words supplemented by a sort of invented mimed language we had experimented with in Burgundy, which we called "grummelotage," or "the music of meaning."

Removed from anecdote and plot, this kind of representation opened the way to a return to the sources of drama and to the creation of an epic theatre at a time, in 1931, when Brecht was quite unknown outside Germany.

But for us a deep, continuing concern remained: in this way of working would the actor and the writer neutralise one another?

As we rehearsed with Obey we dreamed of making our work accessible to a new, much wider audience. Our idea was to set our actors within a bare space under brilliant lights where the audience would be directly exposed to the explosive power of the acting.

Promises

During this time one of the main contributions to the artistic development of my life was the visit to Paris in 1922 of Stanislavski's company, the Moscow Art Theatre. The Russian Revolution was five years old, but the members of the company were still the same as before the Revolution, so that their ensemble playing had not been affected.

Their first performance in Paris of *The Cherry Orchard* filled me with admiration, almost against my will. Nothing had prepared me for the discovery that a banal story about the sale of a country estate could be so moving. Written in an impressionistic style, its silences and long pauses in some way seemed to express the inexpressible.

The deftness of the company's acting was absolutely incredible: without forcing anything, they were alive. They did not seem to touch the ground. Their movements seemed to flow through them, as they communicated freely with one another.

What struck me most was the lightness of their acting: these performers seemed constantly to improvise their movements and their text. Every movement had a prodigious creative invention about it, but nothing seemed ever to solidify; all was ephemeral.

The words, so clearly enunciated, expressed the mood musically; they soared from the actor's mouths. There were fullthroated intonations as well as crystalline modulations, but their musical flexibility never became obvious. There was no straining after truth, nothing was overdone, and yet the smallest reaction was played out fully with realistic precision.

The fluidity of their inner impulses, the rapidity of their reflexes, sustained the actors and made it seem as though they were floating on air. Their performances were an enchantment! At once so moving, and so comic, the dominant impression was poetic, achieved without rhetoric, without lyricism and without solemnity.

That evening Stanislavski played Gaev, an ineffectual, weak

character, a man carrying the relics of his faded past glory. For Gaev, although still superb looking, all that is left to him is empty charm. It was wonderful to watch Stanislavski, who had the stature of a giant, draw upon his physique to establish this empty glamour. He was like a tailor's dummy of long ago.

There was another aspect that contributed to the extraordinary creation of life on the stage: the actors, when entering, brought with them an entire outside world and they had a way, when leaving the stage, of prolonging, of extending the completed action. They were able to make visible the very air around them; they made it *act*. They knew how to make objects come alive, how to make even the furniture breathe.

One of the most astonishing moments was in the first act: the travellers enter, home after a long journey from Paris. Although visibly tired, one feels how moved they all are to find themselves back in the old nursery. Anya, the youngest, a frail creature, runs in, throws herself on the sofa and snuggles into a corner like a little bird. She starts to laugh! That laugh expressed happiness, exhaustion, youth and tenderness. It was a laugh so crystalline, so wonderfully free, with such an emotional impact, that the audience of two thousand people in the Grand Théâtre des Champs Elysées burst into applause, without a word having been uttered from the stage.

Stanislavski's work, so different from Copeau's, was based on psychological realism—impressionist and sensitive. He wanted to represent nature and life directly, trying to produce illusions behind an imaginary fourth wall. To me his attempt failed in the visual realm, where this sort of realism cannot create theatrical illusion.

But in the domain of interpretation, the actors of the Moscow Art Theatre Company succeeded in achieving profound truth. Through his work Stanislavski found a perfect balance between the actors' subjective introspection, their objective study of the characters and their technique of physical action and spoken expression. They arrived at a freedom in acting which I have never seen equalled.

In that respect Stanislavski's achievement confirmed and complemented Copeau's work. The strength of both Copeau and Stanislavski grew out of their rejection of all theatrical artifice. The impression of perfect authenticity generated a feeling of great liveliness which reached across the footlights to the audience. All this, Copeau, in a different artistic perspective, had already succeeded in implanting in his school.

Although we of the Vieux Colombier admired the Moscow Art Theatre's production of *The Cherry Orchard*, the same questions occurred to us all: would these actors, performing so marvelously the poetic realism of Chekhov, be equally convincing if they were to play the great "classics"—the Greek, the Spanish, the French, the Elizabethan? What of Shakespeare, that prototype of non-naturalistic dramatists?

Stanislavski himself wrote in *My Life in Art* about his 1911 production of *Hamlet:* "There was that in the interpretation which we feared most of all—either the usual theatrical pathos or, at the other pole, a very tiresome, heavy and prosaic living of the role. Why could we not find the golden mean?" This artistic problem concerned Stanislavski all his life: "Apparently it still lay before us to go through the same work and find analogical methods and means for plays in the grand heroic style."

I think that the always sincere Stanislavski posed, in a very honest way, the question as to how a system deriving from Chekhovian poetic realism can ever hope to arrive at the same artistic truth when it is applied to Shakespeare.

Stanislavski, a great reformer, authentically "naturalistic," declared: "Our art is founded on the organic basis of the laws of nature." But, to me, a true artist, even from this indisputable basis, can create worlds that have an existence of their own and are not directly governed by the laws of living nature. That artist can create characters, places and languages that exist independently of nature. A Japanese Nō play, Jarry's *Ubu Roi*, the metaphysical theatre of Artaud, Genet's *Balcony*—they all go beyond the natural world. The same is true of a whole realm in Shakespeare, no doubt the part that Stanislavski called "heroic."

But there is a more serious question: when Stanislavski prepared his production of *Othello*, he could not conceive it without detailed research on Venice. He was affected by the geographical reality of the city to such an extent that he had to put real canals and gondolas on the stage! But the world of *Othello* is unique to that play itself; it is a world that cannot be reduced to canals and gondolas, nor to psychological motivations for actors, because it is above all a poetic world. It does not imitate life; it is nourished by reality but rises above it. Its essence is expressed by rhythmic images in a musical language with which a realistic performance, based on rational details, will come into conflict. How would an actor *live* a part that is beyond the natural world? To be truthful, in Shakespeare it is not sufficient to find a "technique of expression." One first has to understand and feel the poetic, the *real* world of Shakespeare, as the realistic and poetic world of Chekhov was understood and felt by Stanislavski.

If Stanislavski's system is applied literally, it leads merely to realism, but applied selectively, with discrimination, it can be made "the grammar of all styles" that it aspires to be.

In the early thirties I found myself in the mainstream of developments in contemporary theatre. I was often in contact with men of the theatre and writers who were beginning new theatrical movements and whose ideas were sometimes antagonistic to those of the Vieux Colombier.

But there were also those who were in the direct lineage of Copeau and who were pursuing similar creative ideas. First of them was Charles Dullin, actor, director, and, later, teacher. Copeau had engaged Dullin to play Smerdiakov in his adaptation of Dostoievski's *The Brothers Karamazov,* which he directed in 1911 at the Vieux Colombier. This was Dullin's first great role and he and Copeau became friends and collaborators for many years.

It was Dullin who was amongst the first directors to revive plays by such Elizabethan and Jacobean playwrights as Webster, Tourneur, Ford and others. He directed plays in a provocative way that attempted to break with traditional forms of realistic expression.

Between the two World Wars Dullin achieved the summit of his acting career with his brilliant portrayal of Volpone in Ben Jonson's play. This, to me, was an unforgettable experience.

There were many followers of Copeau who developed his ideas and in the lineage of Dullin there was Jean Louis Barrault, so unforgettable as the Pierrot in the film *Les Enfants du Paradis.*

In Paris, I was regularly in contact with groups of artists who belonged more or less to Surrealism. In 1932 I met Antonin Artaud who was working with Dullin on the production of Calderon's *Life Is A Dream*. He and I passed the better part of three nights talking together at the Café de la Coupole in Montparnasse.

Artaud had heard about the experiments we had been doing with the Compagnie des Quinze. He wanted to know about our silent improvisations, our search for physical means of expression. He asked about the "grummelotage" we had used in our improvisations and also in some of the plays by Obey.

I explained to him that we felt we needed sound of some sort to sustain the mimed passages and had invented a language of sound—articulation without any apparent logic—which transmitted states of feeling and states of mind by cries, murmurs, and by a kind of chant, all related to the dramatic moment. This, coupled with movement, became a dynamic representation of things and beings in their primordial nature.

Artaud asked his questions avidly. Behind his impatient lucidity I saw in his dark eyes a mysterious anxiety that disturbed me. In our discussions he seemed desperate to have my understanding if not agreement. Much later I found in his writings the following which parallels our conversation:

> Words in the occidental theatre serve to express the psychological conflicts of man and situations in his everyday life . . . However, the domain of theatre is not psychological but plastic, physical. It is not a question of whether the physical "language" of theatre is capable of representing the same psychological states as the language of words, or whether physical language can express feelings and passions as well as words; rather, it is whether there is not in the domain of thought, of intelligence, that which words are incapable of conveying, states which gestures and all that pertains to "language in space" can express with more precision than words.

And then further:

> It is not a question of eliminating the use of words in the theatre, but of giving words approximately the importance

they have in dreams . . . We must manipulate words like solid objects which unsettle things, first in the air, then in the much more mysterious domain of far-reaching influences.

The Compagnie des Quinze re-opened the newly-equipped Théâtre du Vieux Colombier in 1931 with *Noah* and *Le Viol de Lucrèce*, both plays by André Obey. Most of the company were products of Copeau's Vieux Colombier school and had worked together for many years. This long association made for our great strength, but it also contained the seeds of our dissolution.

After these plays had run for three months in Paris, we were invited to perform in London, at the Arts Theatre Club, where we were enthusiastically received by the public and press. Thanks to this first success, the Compagnie des Quinze returned to London annually for four years for a three- to four-week season, the last being in 1934. We also toured in Belgium, Germany and French Switzerland.

In 1933, the Compagnie des Quinze was invited to Madrid to open the new theatre at the Ciudad Universitaria, where we played *Le Viol de Lucrèce* and *La Mauvaise Conduite*. We stayed for a week in Madrid and got to know Garcia Lorca, who was then all but unknown outside Spain. His company, La Barraca, was touring Spain bringing to new audiences who had never seen theatre the masterpieces of Spanish dramatic literature. I came to know the world of Lorca's play *Blood Wedding*, which I was later to direct in its first London production. It is written in a poetic, mystical style that has a kind of realistic lyricism expressed in a rhythmic language, close to music. Its images set in motion cosmic forces from which the characters spring, like sparks from a flint, driven by the most profound and the most primitive impulses. A world not without rapport with that of surrealism.

In France, many artists who were vibrant forces in literature and the arts, became our followers and supporters. We made many close friends.

But in spite of considerable success with the public we were, particularly in Paris, considered the "benjamins" of the Vieux Colombier, which was thought of as a "Théâtre d'Art." This reputation hung on; we did not feel free. We continued to be a curiosity. We appealed to the young and to the avant-garde, but we came up against the fundamental fact of French theatre: it is by nature intellectual and by tradition classical.

Discouraged by all this and by the fact that some of the permanent members of our company had left us, we decided to leave Paris and to settle somewhere else where we could start a school and an experimental laboratory.

It was with Jean Giono, a writer to whom I am indebted for discoveries that are still precious to me, and with Darius Milhaud, the composer—both of whom were then living in Provence—that I formed the plan of establishing a centre near Aix-en-Provence, not far from Giono's house in Manosque. We found a beautiful and suitable house called "Beau Manoir" and it was there that we began again.

Giono was an epic novelist, a Provençal poet in the tradition of the Irish and Greek masters. He had written a first play, *Lanceurs de Graines,* and one of his novels, *Le Serpent des Etoiles,* haunted me for a long time; I wanted very much to adapt it into a play to be acted in the open air.

We were able to gather around us a group of talented people to act with the Compagnie des Quinze and teach the students.

Our desire to restore poetic expression to its proper place in the theatre led us to make music an integral part of our work. Milhaud and Kurt Weill were to join us as directors of music for the Company and the school.

The venture in Aix-en-Provence lasted only six months. The company disbanded under pressure of the constant difficulties generated by communal life. And we had no money. The artistic success of the Compagnie des Quinze had not brought the financial compensation due to actors of talent who had selflessly contributed many years of experimental work to the theatre.

In London, from the first appearance of the Compagnie des Quinze at the Arts Theatre in 1931, the public's reaction, the tone of the press, the daily visits we received from leading members of the acting profession, made us feel that the impact of our performances was something more than just an ordinary theatrical success. People of all sorts wanted us to know that they were refreshed by our plays and by our way of acting. They found us direct, real, devoid of artificial brilliance. Although we played in French, there seemed to be no barriers of language. Our performances had a kind of universal language that made them, according to one critic, ". . . a dramatic revelation." Our proficiency seemed to be appreciated: how we blended the written text with mime, dance and song; how we, even while wearing masks or turning cartwheels or risking somersaults in the air, could pass freely and without effort from one mode of expression to another.

The eruption onto the London stage of this anti-naturalistic form of drama demonstrated that a new realism based on action and *physical* expression was possible. This created quite a shock in the West End theatre, then mostly devoted to solid, bourgeois comedy and drama.

Our plays were not based on plots evolved from the detailed psychology of character: they told stories in action, using narrative devices. Most of the time, unconsciously, our style was "epic," before the word came into fashion.

Around us rallied all those artists who were in search of something new and who were slowly to transform the English stage over the next thirty years.

George Bernard Shaw and G.K. Chesterton came to see us perform. The great classical actors John Gielgud, Sybil Thorndike, Laurence Olivier and Edith Evans visited our dressing rooms, as did Michael Redgrave, Peggy Ashcroft, Alec Guinness, Charles Laughton.

Over the years, since my first visit to London, I had come to realise that by tradition as well as temperament the English have a more down-to-earth understanding of theatre than the French—they react directly and sensitively to poetry. They have also a great openness to the physical poetry of objects and people. Shakespeare to them is *alive*—not intellectually—but concretely. Consequently they were much better prepared to accept an art in which psychological, intellectual and literary preoccupations were not the primary considerations. It seemed to me that everything we had been attempting for fourteen years might be accomplished in England.

In London, Marius Goring, who had been with us in Aix-en-Provence during the last period of the Compagnie des Quinze, helped me attempt to raise the necessary money to re-establish our project in Provence—but without success. Maynard Keynes, the eminent economist and great friend of the arts, advised us that our only hope of finding financial help in England would be for an English project.

After many discussions with my former colleagues in the Compagnie des Quinze and with other French and English friends, I finally decided to open a theatre studio in London, in the country that seemed to understand my work best.

I was given the hope of financial support on condition that I settle in London.

Among the many who generously supported me were Tyrone Guthrie, John Gielgud, Laurence Olivier, Marius Goring, Bronson Albery and his wife, Ian E. Black, Laura Dyas, Vera Burton and her husband Basil, and Charles Laughton, who had also helped financially with the last production of the Compagnie des Quinze, Obey's *Don Juan*.

John Gielgud asked me to stage André Obey's *Noah* for him in English. The play was well received but the interpretation lacked something of the vital spirit, the inventiveness, that the production of the Compagnie des Quinze had possessed. This confirmed my feeling that I might have something to contribute to the English theatre. At that time I spoke only elementary English, but I was convinced that my ultimate contribution did not depend entirely on language.

My project for the creation of a theatre studio was taken under the wing of George Devine whom I met at the Motleys', three well-known designers—Sophie Devine, and Percy Harris and Elizabeth Montgomery—who later had considerable influence on theatre design in England. In their studio in St. Martin's Lane, which had been the workshop of Thomas Chippendale, the 18th century cabinetmaker, artists of all kinds gathered every evening.

It was there that Marius Goring introduced me to George Devine and Glen Byam Shaw, who later became my best and life-long friends. It was with them that I worked out the plans for what was to become in 1936 the London Theatre Studio, my first school.

Glen Byam Shaw, Michel Saint-Denis and George Devine. *(Photo: Radio Times Hulton Picture Library.)*

Chapter Two

THE SCHOOLS

LONDON

The London Theatre Studio
1935-1939

Order from disorder sprang.
MILTON, *Paradise Lost*

IN JANUARY, 1936, the London Theatre Studio, familiarly known as the L.T.S., opened the doors of its own home, after a year's work in rented rehearsal studios.

We did not want a school for a school's sake; our guiding lines were clear: we wanted a place for training young actors who, on issuing from the Studio, would form a company. This company would have at its core the best students of the school, students who had been entirely trained by us, but the company would be led, at first, by a few well-known actors, who were sympathetic to our aims.

We intended to equip our young acting students with all the means of expression we used at the Compagnie des Quinze, but we wanted to extend the imaginative, the creative basis of the Quinze's training. It had been a wonderful training but it had, nevertheless, made us specialists of a particular kind.

I realized that the L.T.S. had to go beyond that specialization if it wanted to be in a position to face the problems of interpreting classical and modern plays in all their variety. There were problems I had previously hardly touched upon: among them the technical and artistic development of voice and speech, and, especially, imaginative expression through language.

Our purpose was to enlarge the actor's field of expression and to equip him in such a way that he could put each technique that he learned to the service of his acting without falling into the trap of specialisation in any of them.

We wanted to form an actor who would be able to handle a sword as well as a cup of tea, an actor who would have expressive and imaginative physical and vocal means, an actor whose voice would have the wide range necessary to carry classical and modern texts, rather than one capable of only the jerky, staccato delivery usual in the stock companies of the time.

The main objectives of the L.T.S. were to develop in the student initiative, freedom, and a sense of individual responsibility as well as the ability to merge his individual qualities into an ensemble. Although the acquisition of a strongly developed technique of body and voice was one of our basic aims, technique was never to be allowed to dominate or supersede invention. We were not interested in quick results, we were interested in the gradual growth of each individual talent.

One of the results of working in this careful and relaxed way is the creation of that *climate* of happy freedom and strong discipline which is essential for creative work in the theatre.

As we were not attached to a professional theatre but were going to experiment with new ways of training and new ways of acting and directing, we felt that it was essential to concentrate at first on young talent which was not yet ossified, still free of theatrical bad habits. But we should at the same time open our doors to professional actors who wished to perfect their technique and enlarge their acting experience.

At that time actors began to divide their work between the theatre, radio and films; all this worked against the creation of permanent companies. What we wanted at the L.T.S. was to have a pool of actors at our disposal who would be able to occupy their free time between our plays with work elsewhere. This pool would not consist of established professional actors only, but would have as its principal source a group of students whom we would train and incorporate into the pool.

The amalgamation of the professional actors attached to us and our chosen students would take place in the third year of training when we intended to open a Studio-Theatre with experimental and other kinds of shows.

In order to become a complete theatrical organisation we also had to train directors and designers, to interest authors in writing for us and to provide time for experiments in which there would be a cross-fertilization of dramatist, actor, director and designer.

Of course our first, and most essential, desire was to serve the contemporary theatre; but in order to do this we needed to prepare actors capable of interpreting *all* styles without letting style deflect from truth. Besides developing his physical and vocal technique, we needed to train the student in the constant practice of a wide variety of texts. We were searching for the proper way to give him a sense of creative freedom. Experimentation, the quest for new forms, was our preoccupation.

I had always thought of Shakespeare and the Elizabethans as being particularly close to the spirit of our time; in England, I wanted to find a way to bring to them a freshness, a new vigour, to give them a contemporary reality without corrupting their style or the purity of their language.

In 1935 I felt this all the more, as I had just seen John Gielgud's company in his famous production of *Romeo and Juliet*. Gielgud and Laurence Olivier, playing Romeo and Mercutio, exchanged parts halfway through the run of the play, giving the public an opportunity to compare two very different interpretations.

The staging by Gielgud, with settings by the Motleys, was admirably flexible; the passage of time and changes of place were suggested by rapid modifications of the permanent stage set, effected within full view of the audience and accompanied by music and changes of lighting. This allowed for a fluidity of action which was new at that time. It was one of the most significant productions of pre-war days, an indication of coming change. To me it was an early and brilliant demonstration of that oscillation between the two magnetic poles of all modern theatre: subjective reality and objective consideration of style.

The details of the training will be covered in Chapter Three, but it seems necessary to state here that from the beginning improvisation played the most important part in the work. Improvisation is, as we understand it, a means to discover in oneself the sources of acting, and is a fundamental way to open up new and unexpected horizons for a young actor. We added to the kind of training which had proved invaluable to the Compagnie des Quinze a carefully selected group of Stanislavski's exercises: those which would not lead our actors to an excessively subjective concentration which might prove detrimental in acting a classical role.

We were fortunate to have on the faculty Marius Goring, as teacher/director, and George Devine, who later became the Director of the famous Royal Court Theatre. Devine contributed considerably to the building of our training programme; he also became the managing director of the L.T.S. His great knowledge of English dramatic literature and his specific talent as an actor and director of comedy were invaluable to the development of the training programme.

Darius Milhaud, who had collaborated with us at Aix-en-Provence, suggested that we engage Suria Magito, who later became my wife. He had seen her company and heard her special orchestra of percussion instruments in rehearsals and performances in Paris. Her work combined mime, the use of splendid original Nō masks, speech, chanting and dance. As we had worked along similar lines, Milhaud thought her the very person I needed for the kind of experimental work I contemplated.

We were lucky to find an unused chapel in the north of London, in Islington. It was not far from Collins' Music Hall, a celebrated theatrical "temple" which stood in the midst of architectural surroundings out of a Dickens novel. This chapel was converted to our purposes by the now-famous architect Marcel Breuer. He built there to our specifications a stage, rehearsal rooms, workshops and an elevated cabin at the back of the auditorium where we placed all the necessary controls for lighting and sound. It was a place where the stage manager was king. It was from there that he could command a view of all that was happening on the stage, follow the action and instantly adjust lighting cues or recorded music to the rhythm and the timing of the show while immediately judging their effect. This was an innovation at the time, although it is common practice now in theatre architecture.

Breuer designed the stage and an auditorium which held about 190 seats. By drastically increasing the slope of the auditorium he reduced the distance between the stage and the back of the hall, thereby putting our actors into intimate contact with the audience.

In addition to our acting course, we started an advanced course for professional actors and directors and a technical course for designers and technicians of the theatre. At the head of the design course were the three Motleys.

Actors and writers who had seen the performances of the Compagnie des Quinze came to the Studio and followed our training work closely: Laurence Olivier, Alec Guinness, John Gielgud, Peggy Ashcroft and many others.

We also succeeded in implanting in the training of actors elsewhere our then-unfamiliar notions. Other schools began to give importance to physical training and mime, even if they did not go as far as we had in the practise of improvisation.

In 1938, two years after opening the Studio-School, we were able to present in our own theatre, to an invited audience, a performance in which the acting was the equal of that which the Compagnie des Quinze had produced in France.

In that same year some of our best students were chosen for John Gielgud's newly formed repertory company at the Queens' Theatre in Shaftesbury Avenue.

The performances we gave at the L.T.S. began to attract interested audiences, the press and the general public. The Studio was beginning to make its presence felt in the theatre life of London.

I remember among the most exciting productions at the L.T.S. the *Midsummer Night's Dream* directed by Marius Goring which used some of the Studio's experiments in voice techniques which opened doors to new ways of vocal expression. *The Fair*, a show devised by George Devine and Suria Magito, revealed a tumbling technique seldom possessed by actors. A Restoration play, with an extraordinarily effective perspective decor, was directed by George Devine and acted with style and gusto by the students. Then there was a Nō, performed by Suria Magito wearing an original Japanese Nō mask of a witch and accompanied by an orchestra of percussion instruments, which created a stunning impression. *Judith,* an adaptation of the apocryphal story by Carl Wildman, was directed by me. In it, the archaic presentation of the speaking chorus, with its absolute physical stillness set off by the solo performer in her loneliness, had a moving vitality which affected the audience deeply.

These were exciting years of experimentation, of trial and error, that were to leave, in many ways, their mark on the theatrical life of England.

All this was engulfed in the furnace of war. I was to be away from the theatre for six years. Part of this time I served in the French Army. After the German invasion of France, I escaped to England via the disastrous Dunkirk escape route in June, 1940. The Foreign Service of the BBC enlisted me, under the pseudonym Jacques Duchesne, as Head of the French Section Foreign Broadcasts. Thus I spent the war years in London.

My theatre work in London was, miraculously, taken up again in 1945 when I directed Laurence Olivier in *Oedipus Rex* for the Old Vic Company, a production which was later taken to New York. Then there was the founding of the Old Vic Theatre Centre, with its School and Company, "The Young Vic," and then, later on, the work with the Royal Shakespeare Company at Stratford-upon-Avon, with, at first, Glen Byam Shaw and Anthony Quayle, and, later, Peter Hall, Peter Brook and myself as Directors. All this was connected in spirit with our pre-war efforts, as was George Devine's work at the Royal Court.

The Old Vic Theatre Centre

The Old Vic Theatre School
The Young Vic Company
1947-1952

A school is a place to re-invent theatre.

THE IDEA FOR the Old Vic Theatre Centre came out of one of those long periods of brooding which are usually forced upon us by

Laurence Olivier in the Old Vic Company's production of *Oedipus Rex*, directed by Michel Saint-Denis. *(Photo: John Vickers.)*

Powys Thomas and Anne Morrish as the ravens in the Young Vic Company's production of Hans Christian Andersen's *The Snow Queen*, directed by Suria Saint-Denis. *(Photo: Keystone Press Agency, Ltd.)*

war. Years of catastrophe and frustration often spur on to action those whom such an ordeal has not destroyed. When survivors are re-united, especially within a profession like that of the theatre, their first reaction is to see whether they cannot do something together, something better and more effective, if possible, than what they were doing before they were parted.

This then was the background of our lives in 1944. It was an era of new planning for the theatre and the arts.

The Board of Governors of the Old Vic Theatre in London began to consider many ideas for the re-shaping of its policies and it was decided to form a permanent repertory company under the joint directorship of Laurence Olivier, Ralph Richardson and John Burrell.

At the same time I proposed to the Board a plan: to establish a training centre under the mantle of the Old Vic.

While we were waiting for the Board's decision, I earned my living by writing articles for the BBC. In 1945 I went on a much-needed holiday to France. There I had my first heart attack. This kept me away from London for five months.

My plan was accepted by the Board. I returned to London and was appointed General Director of the Centre. I became responsible for its overall policies.

The Old Vic Theatre Centre, as it was called, was to be composed of a school—the Old Vic Theatre School—with Glen Byam Shaw as its Head, a young touring company—called the Young Vic—which would work under George Devine with Suria Saint-Denis as Co-Director and an experimental group, which would be run by all of us jointly. This last venture, alas, never came into being.

It was my conviction that a liaison with a professional company, playing a wide-ranging repertoire of classical and modern plays, was indispensable to the existence of a *total* school.

For the re-building of the Old Vic Theatre's stage, which had been badly damaged by bombs during the War, the Board agreed that we employ Pierre Sonrel, the renowned French theatre architect. This reconstruction was a very important element in our plans. We wanted to modernize the stage and put into practice new thinking about theatre architecture: the essence of which, to me, is instrinsically linked to any kind of change in the theatre, to new developments in playwriting, acting and staging.

The Old Vic, one of the finest permanent professional acting companies in the English-speaking world of that time, had built a great reputation by its tours in Great Britain and elsewhere in the world.

In England before World War II it was the comfortable middle classes who sent their sons and daughters to drama schools—they could afford the fees. But after the war the educational authorities in many cities began giving grants to young people with talent for acting. This meant that a less intellectual, sometimes even less educated, talent had access to the drama schools. This was to be a very important factor in the evolution of the theatre in the post-war years, one which gave it fresh strength and colour.

In response to our first announcement and brochure we had over five hundred applications; after exacting auditions we chose a group of twenty-five acting students for the school.

For the auditions the applicants were asked to present two scenes from a list of classical and modern plays selected by us. In addition they might perform a scene of their own choice. When in doubt we would sometimes ask the applicant to improvise, without words, a short scenario on the spur of the moment or with, perhaps, five minutes of preparation. Sometimes a student would be accepted on the strength of his improvisation. In order to get the "feel" of each applicant the audition committee would talk with him individually for twenty- or twenty-five minutes. This procedure proved invaluable in recognising students with real talent, personality and presence.

Concerning the training, the Old Vic Theatre School differed from the London Theatre Studio in several ways: the main line here was to be an approach to an organic training, in all its branches, with constant attention to the interrelation between the various parts of the teaching. I intended also to develop much further the teaching of voice-speech-language and adopt a far more imaginative approach to speech than we had had time to develop in the short life of the L.T.S. As I was sure of the value of improvisation in the development of the actor's physical imagination, I felt that similarly we ought to find new ways to train the vocal imagination of the actor.

We had also to find a new way to bring *reality* to the interpretation of all theatrical styles, particularly the classical styles, without letting that reality destroy the form of the writing. By doing so the students would achieve the greatest possible freedom in their practice and be able to play anything demanded of them—Shakespeare and Chekhov, Ibsen and O'Neill, Noel Coward as well as Marlowe and Sheridan.

The task of rejuvenating Shakespearian acting seemed to me more and more crucial if one was to bridge the growing gap between conventional and modern staging. At the Old Vic Theatre Centre and its school I had the broadest field in which to explore and realize ideas about the training of actors.

This then was our aim and ambition: to build up a consistent, continuous theatrical unit for the Old Vic in which the emphasis was on youth and enterprise. We founded a school with a limited number of students so as to be able to train them as responsible individuals.

Working in experimental plays, or shows specially written for the students, would allow them to contribute to the evolution of new theatrical forms; the experimental stage would be a place where such experiments could take place without having to succeed. The right to fail, after all, is a basic element of that climate in which freedom for experimentation can grow.

Another aim of the school was to start a Production Course, in which we would train technicians in stage-management, lighting, production, design and other allied crafts.

As before at the L.T.S., our intention was to serve contemporary theatre. But to prepare for that, the training had to be based on the interpretation of the classics, which better than any other preparation for the theatre of today, gives a modern actor flexibility and creative freedom.

Surrounded as I was by talented and receptive collaborators, I was able to establish with them over the years a way of working that proved then and later invaluable both to the students and to us, their teachers.

In addition to his administrative duties as Head of the school, Glen Byam Shaw made significant contributions to the training, the speech training in particular. He also had an infallible ability to recognise talent and to cast students in roles that would stretch their capabilities and enlarge the scope of their acting.

George Devine, who had represented us at all the meetings of the Old Vic's Board of Governors, took on some teaching as well. He was an indefatigable worker and without him and Glen Byam Shaw the Old Vic Theatre Centre, the Young Vic and the school could not have come into being.

I was fortunate in all my collaborators during that period, who with their imagination and devotion to the work helped to build up the school. We will encounter them in later pages of this book: Marian Watson, Head of the Speech Department, Jani Strasser, Head of Voice, Geraldine Alford, Litz Pisk, Barbara Goodwin, the directors John Blatchley, Pierre Lefèvre and, later, Norman Ayrton and Jeremy Geidt. On the Production Course side there were Stephen Doncaster, the designer, Peter Streuli and Clemence Glock.

In 1947 the school was able to move into the Old Vic Theatre in Waterloo Road which had been scantily repaired and was still unheated. In the bombed-out auditorium, we found a great mound of coal; we spent the first few days with the students removing it and trying to make the place more or less habitable and fit to rehearse in. It was indescribably cold, but everybody was eager and cheerful and the work began.

In 1949 we had to give the theatre over to the architect and builders. We then moved to premises in Dulwich, a part of London widely known for its schools, colleges and museums. There, in its own small theatre, the school gave its public performances to packed houses for two or three weeks every year.

For all of us who worked at the school, this was an extremely fruitful period.

The official opening of the rebuilt auditorium and stage of the Old Vic Theatre took place in 1950. Laurence Olivier gave a memorable speech to the actors and guests, addressing, in particular, the students: "The growth of your career should be like that of a tree, a simple, steady, all round growth. . . . An actor, above all, must be a great understander, either by intuition or observation or both, and that puts him on a level with a doctor, a priest or a philosopher. . . . If I can get more from him [the actor] than just belief, then I feel both fortunate and overjoyed. . . . You will not finish learning until you are dead."

After only five years of operation, the life of the Old Vic Theatre Centre was brusquely brought to a halt, on the pretext that the Centre cost too much money and that the Arts Council of Great Britain, which also provided funds for the Old Vic Company and its dependent organisations, needed the money to pay off the debts of the Old Vic's professional company. The Centre was dissolved, and with it the school and the Young Vic.

This Centre, to which a devoted group of professional people had given their time and their energy and for which they had given up their personal careers, was cut off just as it began to be fruitful.

Valiant efforts were made by our friends to save at least the school, but, to our indignation and disappointment, the obstacles proved too great and so we parted and the Faculty, loyal to the end, dispersed.

In 1952 I decided to leave London in spite of tempting offers from West End theatre managers. With my wife, Suria, I left for France to start again.

STRASBOURG, FRANCE

L'Ecole Supérieure d'Art Dramatique

1952-1957

> Do not confine your children to your own learning— for they were born in another time.
> HEBRAIC SAYING

AS THIS WAS TO BE the third school I had planned, it would not be unreasonable for the reader to ask "Is he obsessed by the idea of training actors? What *is* it that drives him so?" Somehow my life seems curiously composed of periods of five to six years; every five or six years I start again from zero. I recover my breath and fate invites me to go on. This seems hard, but perhaps it is necessary if one is not to live in the stagnation of one's ideas.

There were very deep reasons why I felt that a place for the formation of young actors should be established in France. In our era (and mine started in 1913—at the age of sixteen!) a movement in the theatre was born which felt the necessity to search for *truth* in the interpretation of classical plays and to create a new theatrical ambiance. It was based on a desire to restore to the theatre its vocation of being not only a place of entertainment, but also a place where there is communion with the play: communion between man and man. At that time the staging of plays became more and more simplified, so that the *text* could reveal its true merit.

In 1913 there were beginning to be changes in the architecture of the stage and, here and there, the stage was already being brought forward towards the auditorium. In order to kill the artifice of lighting, footlights disappeared; lighting began to *suggest* rather than to illustrate. And, above all, efforts were made to destroy those routines of the actors which had taken the place of life. While respecting the conventions of the stage, which, in general, require enlargement of sound and gesture, actors had begun to search for deeper revelations and were attempting to achieve as incisive a reality as possible.

But very quickly it was found that, on the stage, truth alone is not sufficient. Even if an actor possesses sincerity, he often does not have the technical means to convey that sincerity.

It became necessary to develop both the actor's imagination and his technique. These techniques were then called new, but they were not really new at all, if we consider the technique of a Greek actor or a Japanese Nō actor or even an actor of the Commedia dell' Arte, or of the time of Molière, Racine or Shakespeare. Nor were they new when one takes into account the techniques developed by dancers, musicians and singers over the years. Considering this, one became convinced that in order to liberate theatre it was necessary to add new branches of training; sincerity alone is not sufficient, just as in science invention without technique is not enough.

In the period after the Second World War, in many sectors of the theatrical field in France, there was great activity. The Ministry of National Education (which later became, under André Malraux, the Ministry of Cultural Affairs) had at the head of its Theatre Department the imaginative Jeanne Laurent, who wanted to decentralise the Arts by establishing five regional art centres, each with a theatre as well as halls for concerts and exhibitions. They were all to be under one roof. They were to have permanent theatre companies and, ideally, training schools for all the Arts.

This then-new idea was taken up subsequently in many other countries of the world.

In 1952 I was appointed General Director of the Centre for the eastern region of France—in Strasbourg—the seat of the Council of Europe.

The municipality of Strasbourg constructed, with substantial help from the Government, a specially designed building in the middle of this beautiful, medieval city. Once again, Pierre Sonrel was our architect. Part of the building was to house the well-known Conservatoire de Musique de Strasbourg and l'Orchestre Symphonique de Strasbourg under the famous conductor Charles Munch. The rest of the building was to house the Ecole d'Art Dramatique.

There were two professional touring companies which had their headquarters at the Centre, where all their shows were rehearsed and prepared.

These companies toured the region extensively throughout the year. Each company consisted of fifteen actors made up of our own former students and professional actors recruited from Paris.

Professional actors at that time were willing to join our company which was some distance from Paris in order to avail themselves of its very real advantages: year round work under able directors, and immensely receptive audiences. The companies had a fine new theatre of their own. The fact that this theatre was in the same building as the school, and that the students were living in the atmosphere and under the eye, as it were, of the profession, was of great advantage to both students and actors. The actors became aware of the importance of such training and the students, who could watch a permanent company functioning, with all that this entails in rehearsals and the preparation of its shows, came in touch with the realities of their future lives.

The school was directed and administered by Suria Saint-Denis, who also taught improvisation and mask-work and directed shows for the two companies.

It was possible to have from the beginning an experienced faculty because four of my former teachers at the Old Vic Theatre School in London had asked to join us: Jani Strasser became head of the Voice Department and Barbara Goodwin taught movement and, later, improvisation. Pierre Lefèvre, one of my former students at the London Theatre Studio, who then taught at the Old Vic Theatre School and acted in the Young Vic Company, taught acting and improvisation and also directed shows for the company. The fourth was John Blatchley, who for several years was Assistant Director to Glen Byam Shaw at the Old Vic Theatre School.

The design course had at its head Abdel Farrah, a very gifted, imaginative painter, set and costume designer who was, as well, a brilliant teacher. He subsequently became resident designer for the Royal Shakespeare Company in Stratford-upon-Avon, England.

The rest of the faculty was either local, like the excellent voice and speech teacher André Ross, or from Paris, like the now-well-known director, Daniel Leveugle.

In 1957 I had to resign from the Centre due to ill health. My wife and I returned to London.

The Centre and its School and companies continued under the expert direction of Hubert Gignoux; Pierre Lefèvre succeeded Suria Saint-Denis as head of the School, where he stayed for several years.

CANADA

The National Theatre School of Canada
L'Ecole Nationale de Théâtre du Canada
1960

> If you can look into the seeds of time and say
> which grain will grow, and which will not. . .
> *Macbeth*

THERE IS A TIME in the life of a man and in the development of an artist when, because of the experience he has acquired and because of his desire to be partially disengaged from life—from too much absorbing action—he is brought to try to understand the human adventure, so that he may consider his art and evaluate quietly what he has accomplished. At such times he begins to be aware of his life's underlying philosophy and to recognise and sort out the various means he has employed to give it form. If you like, he establishes a sort of idea-after-action, which can give him a broader, a quieter view of the world.

This artistic adventure, which every artist has got to go through, cannot be separated from the human adventure. What one says, what one does, is what one is.

I must confess that life seems to me tolerable only if it is a constantly-renewed adventure, an adventure in which one can produce, create, search, love, succeed and, sometimes, fail. All this leads one to a great conquest; it leads one to the richest sort of freedom. By which I mean it leads to the mastery of oneself—something very difficult to achieve.

For me, one of these periods occurred in 1952 during one of my several visits to Canada as the final adjudicator of the Dominion Drama Festival Competitions. During three previous visits, while adjudicating for the Festival, I had been struck by the amount of amateur theatre activity there and the budding but untrained talent I encountered in both actors and directors.

Prior to the Second World War most of the theatre in English-speaking Canada was served by either touring companies from England and America or by local amateur theatres, although a few of the major cities, such as Toronto and Montreal, had their own professional companies.

French Canada, centered in Quebec and Montreal, also received visiting companies from France. For most Canadian communities, however, the opportunity to see a live play on the stage, on a professional level, was rare.

The Dominion Drama Festival had come into being in response to the need of local English- and French-speaking companies throughout Canada to communicate.

Once the Festival was established, groups sprang up all over Canada and competitive festivals were held in a different region each year.

In 1952 I was approached by representatives of several Drama League organisations and asked if I would remain in Canada for a year or so to help develop an idea for a professional theatre school. At that time I was unable to remain in Canada, having committed myself to work in France, but five years later my friends approached me again and I agreed to come to Canada to discuss the establishment of a professional training school for actors and directors, with the understanding that I would not be able to run such a school but would give advice and guidance.

During this meeting with the committee, headed by Mrs. Pauline McGibbon, three ideas emerged: 1) that a professional theatre school should be established and that it should follow training principles set forth by me, adapted to suit conditions in Canada; 2) the school should be bilingual, or rather co-lingual, providing under one roof training in all phases of the theatrical arts for both English- and French-speaking students; 3) that it should be a *national* school and situated in Montreal.

Such a bold undertaking could not have happened in any other country but Canada: there existed there a great diversity of cultures owing to immigration from all over Europe. But Canada, unlike the United States, has never been a "melting pot." In Canada the immigrants have in many cases kept their identity, maintaining their own traditions. At the proposed school we hoped to enrich and inspire the students by a close confrontation with cultures other than their own. This had immense possibilities.

Because of my own artistic adventure—having been transplanted from France to England and having absorbed and been enriched by the blending of both cultures—the prospect of helping to prepare a training ground for young actors under such circumstances became a very exciting challenge.

Canada, in order to meet the demands of its growing theatre, had to train its own artists—actors, directors, designers and theatre technicians. No longer could this be adequately done by sending its students abroad to England, America or France.

It was hoped that in time the school would be completely Canadian, run by Canadians for Canadians—whether French- or English-speaking.

The search for a suitable faculty began, and so did the recruiting of students.

The auditions for students were held in major cities all across Canada. No formal academic qualifications were required, but every candidate had to have a proficiency in either English or French. The school was to admit no more than about fifty acting students each year, equally divided between the two language groups. The school was not compelled to accept students from the various regions on a quota basis; students were chosen solely on the basis of talent.

Besides offering courses in Acting and Technical Production, the school hoped to attach one or two promising playwrights to it for a period of one or two years. The school would not give a formal course in playwriting, but prospective writers could be enrolled as students and be free to participate in most branches of the school's activity. They would be encouraged to write class exercises and experimental scenes for the acting students. It was hoped that watching actors and directors at work would contribute to their development as playwrights.

My philosophy of training was accepted as a basis for the different courses.

As I had to leave for Paris, Suria Saint-Denis stayed behind in Montreal for several months to brief the first directors and teachers of the school and to help set up the curriculum.

Jean Gascon, Canada's leading man of the theatre, founder

and director of the Théâtre du Nouveau Monde, became its first Executive Director with James Domville, also Canadian, as its Administrative Director. He was succeeded by Jean Pol Britte, who, with the inspired singing teacher Louis Sprizer, has spent many years with the school. Powys Thomas, a former student of mine in London, and a member of the Old Vic Theatre Company, became the first Head of the English Section. Jean Pierre Ronfard was the first Head of the French Section. The Technical Production Course was headed by David Peacock, formerly stage director at the Covent Garden Opera House in London.

This devoted group of people went through many vicissitudes during the first years of the school's existence. The staff was often faced with enormous financial difficulties and had, sometimes, to spend their own money to help the school or provide grants for needy students.

In the beginning the plan was to teach certain disciplines by bringing the French- and English-speaking students into the same classes—this was possible, of course, only where language was not of primary importance in such classes as movement, singing and silent improvisation. The singing teacher believed strongly, as I do, in teaching singing in both the English and French languages; even if the students were not able to speak one another's language, he felt that this practice would be beneficial to all.

It was, of course, essential for the student to see acting in both languages in the professional theatre. Although there were a number of French-speaking companies in Montreal, at the time of the opening of the school there were hardly any English-speaking theatre companies. So it was planned to take the whole school, students and faculty, to Stratford, Ontario, for two or three months every summer. While the students' basic training continued during the day, in the evening they could attend performances of the professional company at the Festival Theatre. Arrangements were also made for the students to meet with the actors of the company for informal discussions on acting. Unfortunately this was only done for the first few years, as it proved too costly.

The existence of such a total school of theatre will be justified only if it serves the needs of the developing theatre of Canada.

By training young professional artists, the National Theatre School will, I believe, contribute on many levels to the life of the theatre in Canada and will have a profound influence on its artistic climate.

EDITOR'S NOTE

This prophecy has since proved right. Many of the National Theatre School's former students are now working all over Canada in prominent theatres as actors, directors, designers and theatre technicians.

NEW YORK

The Juilliard School Drama Division*
1968-

> What's past is prologue.
> *The Tempest*

THE LINCOLN CENTER PROJECT was set up to investigate the possibility of establishing a complete arts center consisting of an opera house, a ballet theatre, a concert hall and a repertory theatre, as well as a building to house an educational facility for all the performing arts.

The Juilliard School was chosen to administer this facility, with the understanding that it would expand its own field of music and dance to include drama.

In 1956 while I was still the General Director of the Centre Dramatique de l'Est in Strasbourg, we received a visit from a distinguished group of people from America. Led by John D. Rockefeller 3rd, President of the Lincoln Center Project in New York, the spearhead planners for the project, Mr. Anthony Bliss,

*From papers written between 1959 and 1968

President of the Metropolitan Opera, Mr. Wallace K. Harrison, the architect, and Mr. A. L. Fowler, were on a tour of Europe to see the architecture of new theatres, opera houses and concert halls in Germany, France and England.

Robert Chapman, professor of English at Harvard University, who had done research work with a grant from the Rockefeller Foundation on new theatre buildings and drama schools in the United States and Europe, recommended that Mr. Rockefeller and his associates visit Strasbourg in order to meet me and see the new theatre and school complex there.

They stayed for several days in Strasbourg, attending classes at the school and questioning the teachers until they had a good idea of the training. We met several times over lunches and dinners to discuss ways and means to establish a Drama Department at the new Juilliard School at Lincoln Center.

These interesting and cordial meetings ended with Mr. Rockefeller inviting me to visit New York for further consultations.

In 1958 on my first arrival in New York, I was asked by the President of the Juilliard School, William Schuman, to prepare a plan for a *professional* drama school of an advanced kind.

As I had never been in the States before, I was anxious to get to know the country, to learn as much as possible about its attitude towards the theatre—Broadway as well as the educational organisations throughout the country where students are trained for the theatre.

For me, a European, it was surprising to find that, apart from a few professional schools in New York and other cities, theatre, in its theoretical and practical aspects, was being taught primarily in Drama Departments of colleges and universities.

It was therefore of paramount importance that I visit the main universities that had such departments. The Dean of Juilliard, Mark Schubart, set up an itinerary for me and so it was that in February, 1959, I set out, with Suria Saint-Denis, on a coast-to-coast tour.

We saw heads of departments, went into classrooms and community theatres, studied their training methods and performances and talked to scores of students and teachers.

I soon realized that the teaching of theatre in many colleges and universities is part of the liberal arts programme, whose aims

may vary to a degree, but which usually have the common purpose of forming well-educated American citizens. Theatre was
definitely a contributory factor to a liberal arts education; it was
not professionally oriented.

On the valuable side of this training was the recognition of
theatre as a means of education and the acceptance of it as an
art. The diffusion of this notion has contributed to the formation
of a growing theatre public in the United States.

Above all, there was an extraordinary amount of experimentation in the architectural development of new theatres. Many of
these buildings are wonderfully equipped technically and offer
a great variety of stages, from theatre in the round to the arena,
apron and picture-frame stages; some have transformable pro-
sceniums, which allow for every possible theatre convention, classical or modern. Students in the technical courses of most of these
Theatre Departments know how to set a stage, how to light it,
and how, to a certain extent, to build scenery and paint it. The
technical training in all its branches seemed to be very efficient.

But I am not sure that this technical efficiency does not often
destroy spontaneity in creative design; the results are sometimes
more competent than original.

As to the training in acting, it did not, on the whole, seem to
aim at professionalism. The general attitude was that the universities should not prepare students for the profession, but that
the training should definitely remain academic.

However, depending on the attitudes of the teaching faculty
in these Drama Departments, some of them attempted to cut the
liberal arts or academic programme as much as possible and go
farther in practical actor-training.

The approach to theatre training, in general, seemed to be
founded on Stanislavski, or the American "Method." Based on
realism, the training was sometimes classical but realism was always predominant. However, what was being used in these
classes was often a mere version of Stanislavski or classical training, as understood by the teacher. The existence of "method" is
useful as a reference; it gives guidance, but tends, at the same
time, to dampen initiative in teachers and students alike. The
training seemed to consist primarily of discussions and explanations about acting and various theories of acting; it struck me

as a bit too abstract, too intellectual. This sort of discussion makes a young actor much too *conscious* of the problems of acting instead of inducing him to *experience* acting with spontaneity. I often had the feeling that teachers were training other teachers rather than actors.

A complete divorce seemed to exist between style and realism. In plays of pre-realistic periods, style was generally added on later after a "Stanislavskian" preparation.

In any case, because of the emphasis on academic matters, somewhat foreign to a theatre curriculum, seldom did I find enough time given to the indispensable work on essential techniques necessary for a student concentrating on acting.

The conclusions to be drawn from this brief analysis were clear, even if they presented many problems.

I had been asked to plan a professional, advanced school of theatre. If by advanced it was meant that the proposed school would deal with already trained actors from universities and professional theatre schools, all we could hope to do would be to complete the lengthy training such actors had already received and attempt to bring some sort of unity to their varied ways of acting.

However, it seemed clear to me that the new Drama Division of the Juilliard School could only develop originality in acting if it could train its own actors from the very beginning: only by doing so could the school offer a unified way of acting and have a chance to prove itself to be of a truly advanced kind.

In a 1957 statement to the press, John D. Rockefeller 3rd said: "The inclusion of the Juilliard School in Lincoln Center for the Performing Arts is a milestone of major importance in the development of the Center. There is no question that the Center can offer extraordinary opportunities for talented young people desiring advanced training in the performing arts. But equally important is the fact that these young performers and creative artists can and will add immeasurably to the Center as a whole. Association by the seasoned professional with able students will be stimulating, provocative and immensely rewarding. The ability of a school to experiment and to undertake new productions will contribute substantially to the development and advancement in the several fields of the performing arts."

In 1959 William Schuman officially appointed me chief consultant to the projected Drama Division of the Juilliard School and asked me to organise the new division. This would be housed in a building at Lincoln Center when the school moved there from its old headquarters on Claremont Avenue.

In addition to planning the new division, I was also asked to work in close collaboration with Pietro Belluschi, the architect for the new Juilliard building. Consequently I attended the architects' meetings and was consulted on numerous technical questions: on the building of the new stages for the two theatres, their shape, size, sight lines, and on details of the auditoriums, dressing rooms, rehearsal space and classrooms.

I commuted between London, where I was still attached to the Royal Shakespeare Company, and Paris, where I continued to serve as Inspecteur Général des Spectacles, and New York. I also visited some of the newly built theatres in Germany with Mr. Helǧe Westerman, another Juilliard architect. These theatres represented the most interesting current ideas about theatre architecture since World War II.

During my visits to New York I presented my plans for the Drama Division to William Schuman and Mark Schubart. I understood that I had been chosen as consultant because during all my working life in the theatre I had dealt with both the realistic plays of our times and with plays of style from many different countries, particularly France and England. From the beginning, in our conversations a great deal of thought was given to the relation between reality and style.

At Juilliard I found myself confronted with one of the most exciting challenges of my life. I was faced with a new country which offered great possibilities for the establishment of something valid. I was associated with extremely willing people who were in possession of means to achieve our visionary plans. Of equal importance, there existed talented young people to take part in this exciting venture. But for me there were also many problems to consider, problems far more complex than those I had had to face in Europe.

One of the problems was the lack of a long-established tradition in the States. Others were the widespread conventional ideas about prestige and the necessity for financial success.

There was, too, a very uneven diffusion of real culture and theatrical practice around the country. This would, I believed, prove to be one of our more serious problems, as the lack of a unified culture could not help but hinder the development of the young actor/artists.

My own feelings in this were confirmed by knowledgeable people I met in America with whom I had lengthy discussions.

In considering how to organise the training to suit the American scene, it seemed vital to adopt a few basic guidelines. One of the first principles was that the selection of the students should be very severe; acceptance to the Juilliard School should in itself be a distinction. The school would be for a selected, *talented,* few; there would be no interest in mass education. No talented person would be prevented from entering the school for lack of money, and, conversely, money would not prevail over lack of talent. It was expected that, once accepted, after a year of trial, the student would stay through the four-year course. Quality and standards depend on continuity and permanence. Each group entering the school would be kept together from year to year becoming, in effect, a small company. Through that intimate knowledge of one another which grows with constant collaboration over a considerable length of time, students can create a theatre that can promise and realise the best.

Individual talent must, of course, be cultivated but with the constant aim of its contributing to an ensemble.

It was hoped that the great interest of the students in their work would cause them to accept these conditions freely.

At that time Robert Whitehead, of the eminent Broadway producing team Robert Whitehead and Roger Stevens, was appointed Director of the Lincoln Center Repertory Theatre. He understood the concept of an ensemble company and the necessity of training young actors for it. My wife and I respected his views and knowledge of the American scene, had many discussions with him and often sought his advice and help. This relationship grew into a warm friendship.

Whitehead and I devised a plan to link the Juilliard Drama

Division and the Repertory Company. We felt that in order to build this organic relationship the directors of the school and the theatre should be jointly responsible for all aesthetic decisions relating to the training programme. The finances of each institution, however, would be totally separate, so as to prevent the school from being "plundered" should the theatre face economic problems.

In order to define this plan in all its aspects, a meeting was organised with John D. Rockefeller 3rd, William Schuman, Mark Schubart, key members of the Juilliard and Lincoln Center Boards, Robert Whitehead and myself. We presented our plan and discussed the interrelationship of the school and the theatre.

We hoped that this cooperation between the two organisations would ultimately give birth to one of the world's truly great theatres.

I explained that a school of the kind planned for Juilliard should not exist in isolation—it could easily become introverted and lose sight of the realities of professional life. I stressed too that the actors from the Repertory Theatre might also find it profitable, from time to time, to return to the school to improve or develop one or another aspect of their talent.

Whitehead later decided to run the Repertory Theatre on his own, in conjunction with his co-director Elia Kazan. Whitehead hoped that eventually a close interchange would establish itself by Juilliard graduating students joining the company.

But in any event the Vivian Beaumont Theatre, as it was called then, would never be able to absorb all the graduating students coming out every summer. Our aim was also to connect the school with Broadway and the theatre in the rest of the country. To facilitate this we would have to keep in touch with developments everywhere.

Although an American theatrical tradition of a sort has existed since the turn of the century, it needs to develop. It seems to me that one of the main purposes of a school could be to contribute to this development. If this aim were incorporated into the philosophy of the school and the marriage between realism and style, between the modern and the old, brought about through creative, experimental leadership, a truly American tradition of acting and staging, of designing and writing could come about.

But this "marriage" must be made on American terms: the language is English, but as spoken by Americans; the tradition being formed is related by language to the English tradition but it must evolve on its own. If Shakespeare is studied—as, of course, he must be—his meaning for Americans cannot be what it is for the English.

It seems to me that for the development of an American tradition, Shakespeare and the Elizabethans should be only part of the study. Other influences should be considered, perhaps those of the Spanish Golden Age, the unique 17th and 18th centuries in France, the Commedia dell'Arte as well as the eternal lessons of the Greeks and of the Italian Renaissance.

To be truly alive, a school should, while attracting to itself students of the most diverse temperament and character, limit the number of students so that their qualities can be developed to the fullest and the very best be derived from this richness of talent.

We should normally take in about twenty to twenty-five students each year for the acting courses. We would probably have to eliminate three or four of them at the end of the first term and some others at the end of the first year.

Apart from the regular students, there should be what we call an Advanced Course for young professionals who have worked in the theatre as actors but who want to take additional, concentrated training in the various acting disciplines.

The young professionals, who are accepted for the Advanced Course by auditions and personal interviews, would go through an intense two-year course. In their first year they would take part in all the disciplines of the main four-year course, with special individual coaching in whatever area they required. They would also be cast in the plays that would be presented to the public.

In their second year, members of the Advanced Course would join with the fourth-year students to form a Juilliard Acting Company. The members of this company, while continuing their training, would devote most of their time to rehearsing plays to be performed publicly in the school's theatre and on tour in universities and colleges.

The school should also take advantage of the solid work done in the technical courses of the universities and establish an advanced Production Course for the further training of these students in a professional and creative way. This course would last between two and four years and would train students not only for the theatre, but also for the opera and dance.

When, in 1959, my plan for the Juilliard Drama Division was accepted I made it clear that I would not become the Director of the school, as I was convinced that the school should have an American at its head. I *would*, however, be available for consultation, planning, setting up the curriculum and for some teaching, directing and lecturing. To head the school two or three people with whom I had had discussions on the subject of training were recommended.

However, by that time it had become increasingly clear that the Lincoln Center construction programme was going to be delayed for a good many years, and so I returned to Europe and my work there.

In 1965 I was once again approached, this time by the new President of the Juilliard School, Peter Mennin, who came to England to see me at Stratford-upon-Avon. He brought with him the architectural blueprints for the new building and also all the plans I had made for the Juilliard Drama Division's curriculum.

He seemed to be a very determined person and took a great personal interest in getting the Drama Division started. He asked me if I would take on the directorship when it opened, as he hoped, in 1968. I again pointed out that I was convinced that the director should be an American. After long consideration of the people suggested previously, our choice fell on John Houseman, the well-known producer and director, who at that time was the Director of the Shakespeare Festival at Stratford, Connecticut. Peter Mennin then asked me if I would be willing to act as Co-

Director, with my wife as Assistant Director. Because I was very interested in seeing this school come to life and also because I wanted to spend a few years in America, I said I would consider this and let him know as soon as I had studied my commitments in London and Paris.

And so meetings with John Houseman, who was then living in Paris, were arranged.

My wife and I spent some time with him in fruitful discussions and we decided to join him at Juilliard when the Drama Division was ready to open.

As I was not able to be free until the spring of 1968, John Houseman and I agreed to have my wife go over to New York in 1967 and interview a number of people Houseman had in mind for the Juilliard faculty. I could rely on her, as it was she who had found most of the teachers for my other schools.

In the fall of 1967 these interviews took place in New York and the faculty was chosen. It was decided that we would all meet in August of 1968 for an exchange of views on ways of teaching.

John Houseman, with his usual inventive and practical energy, found a delightful country school outside New York where we all foregathered for two weeks. During that time I presented my ideas about training and the interrelationships between all the theatre disciplines and at the same time I got acquainted with the ways the new faculty would teach.

Among that group were many experienced teachers including Stephen Aaron, Michael Kahn, Judith Leibowitz, Peggy Loft-Freed, Marian Seldes, Edith Skinner, Elizabeth Smith, William Woodman, Anna Sokolow and Moni Yakim.

The completion of the new Juilliard building at Lincoln Center had once again been delayed, so in September 1968 we opened in International House, a building just across the way from the old Juilliard School of Music on Claremont Avenue.

EDITOR'S NOTE

In the spring of 1969 Michel Saint-Denis had a stroke and returned to London. He was unable to attend the opening of the Juilliard School in Lincoln Center in September of that year. He did not live to see any of the achievements of the School for which he had worked so hard over so many years; but his philosophy of training actors has been adhered to: his initial vision was followed and developed successfully by John Houseman and his successors Alan Schneider and, later, Michael Langham.

The first Drama Division Administrator was the very capable Margot Harley, subsequently Executive Director of the Juilliard Acting Company.

The faculty Michel Saint-Denis had helped to form has remained together—at the time of this writing—for over eleven years. The members of the original group were joined by such fine directors and teachers as Norman Ayrton, B.H. Barry, Michael Howard, Elizabeth Keen, Jane Kosminsky, Pierre Lefèvre, Gene Lesser, Timothy Monich, Eve Shapiro, John Stix, Harold Stone, Boris Tumarin, John West and Robert Williams.

They have all contributed to making the Juilliard Drama Division a place where students receive their training in an atmosphere of research and invention.

Some outstanding actors who were trained at Juilliard are Tony Azito, Frances Conroy, Benjamin Hendrickson, William Hurt, Kevin Kline, Patti LuPone, Leigh McCloskey, Kenneth Marshall, Elizabeth McGovern, Mandy Patinkin, Christopher Reeve, Norman Snow, David Ogden Stiers and Robin Williams.

The school has become the living proof of the validity of Michel Saint-Denis' vision.

ENGLAND

The Stratford Studio of
The Royal Shakespeare Company
1962

> Every difficulty an actor encounters in his acting can be a stimulus to him.

WHEN I WAS ASKED to join the Royal Shakespeare Company in 1962 as one of its three Directors—with Peter Hall and Peter Brook—my main purpose was to establish a studio for training and experiment which would serve the actors of the Company as well as a specially selected group of ten young actors who would be the nucleus of the Studio.

The Royal Shakespeare Company would provide the premises and administration facilities and the ten young actors would be paid a minimum Equity salary. They would be given special training by qualified teachers in voice-speech-language, in movement and improvisation and in work with masks. At the same time they would do contemporary plays and some experimental work, and they would also be employed as understudies for actors in the main Company and be given small parts in its shows.

Our primary aim was to find new ways to act Shakespeare and the Elizabethans. We wanted to establish a unity of approach among directors; to further this we would have to clarify the new theatrical terms that were then coming into use so that directors and actors would know what was meant when they used such terms as alienation, motivation, "tactile memory," a "Brechtian" or an "Ionesc" (after Ionesco) way of acting.

But our main purpose was to do practical work and experiments which would enlarge the scope of the actor's capabilities.

As the Company was doing mainly Shakespeare at the Stratford theatre, we tried to plunge the Studio members, and any actors of the main company who cared to take part, into many different kinds of plays and different kinds of staging. We worked on thrust stages, in the round and sometimes in the open air.

During these experiments discussions would take place and the meaning of new plays from dramatists such as Brecht, Beckett and Ionesco would, we hoped, be clarified not only by discussion but, more importantly, by *practice* on working on scenes. The actors gradually came to an understanding of then-new trends in playwriting and acting.

We are told that drama gives us a delayed reflection of society. Contemporary drama, I believe, is even more than that: is it not the expression of a world in transformation, the values of which have been corrupted or lost? Hence the anxiety and pessimism of younger dramatists, the suspicion with which they look at their elders, a sharper suspicion, it seems to me, than the natural one between generations. I do not suggest that this situation is good, nor that it creates the conditions of great drama. Their desire for ruthless truth, their passion for lucidity, for analysing reality to the bone, tends to confine the dramatists to the area of daily life, to diminish the scope of their subject matter and to bring expression down to the level of naturalistic mud. "Art," "artistic expression," "form," in this context, become easily synonymous with "artificiality," "rhetoric," "escapism."

The modern theatre in England as well as in France is roughly divided among several movements: there is the neo-realistic, more or less consciously based on Stanislavski, and the epic, which is directly influenced by Brecht. Both of these are generally of a constructive nature with social implications.

There are other movements dealing with the essence of man, of life and of destiny, which make use of the absurd, of psycho-analytical approaches, the subconscious, dreams and allegories. There is here a negation of life and art, and an absence of logic and form.

These movements, when they are not of a destructive nature, often transcend reality and, by representing all aspects of modern anxiety, increase our consciousness of it. They cross each other in the most exciting confusion and have in common a basic sobriety or an unrestrained violence. They are often scornful of the notion of entertainment. They are characterised by moments of lucidity and daring, a pronounced subjectivity, a contempt for beauty and a negation of art for art's sake.

In contrast to these is the mass of the traditional theatre, including that of the Far East.

The traditional theatres, most of the time based on established values, believe in the ability of form and style, whatever the kind, to express the deepest reality or, sometimes, to transcend it.

Today these movements co-exist; sometimes they influence one another but there is little visible or acknowledged exchange. In general there is only antagonism. The new world, being very different from the old, wants to assert itself. The old world, proud, feels the change, attempts to maintain its values but is slowly, albeit reluctantly, obliged to give way.

What I believe to be fortunate in the English theatre is that its basic tradition—the Elizabethan, the Shakespearian tradition—is not too far removed from modern times. There is no real separation: the dramatists of today may reject the most worn-out plots, the period-precious passages, the purely rhetorical speeches, but they do not deny the psychological acuteness, the human illumination which comes out of all Shakespeare's great works. The vision of the world in all its aspects which you receive from Shake-speare amounts to a direct revelation, in which form—what is called poetry—cannot be separated from content. It is one and the same thing. If, as an actor, you do not wed yourself to the verse, then the rational meaning may be there, but the revelation vanishes; at the same time, if you do not, through the text and together with it, search constantly for the reality of meaning and character, then the poetry, empty, disembodied, becomes the too-well-known "music of the words."

At Stratford, with Shakespeare, we are concerned with the highest form of expression in the theatre of today. All over the world, most of Shakespeare's work is recognised as being of the greatest *contemporary* value both from the point of view of meaning as well as form; moreover, in the tradition of the great styles (Greek, Far Eastern, Spanish, Italian and French), it is the only one that continues as a commercial attraction of both popular and international importance. The understanding, sympathy and communication between the Elizabethan world and our own has been manifest for some time. But Shakespeare is not alone: he has emerged from an Elizabethan world crowded with dramatists and poets.

Attempts have been made in some European countries over the last fifty years to perform the Elizabethans in such a way that their subject matter, their mode of composition, their poetry and style could bring inspiration and nourishment to contemporary audiences and artists alike: Elizabethan dramatists were adopted by the Surrealists; Brecht took from them, as well as from Chinese and Japanese theatres, his kind of narrative and part of his style in composition. Because of inadequate translations, however, for-eign attempts have not been able to give powerful enough rev-elations of Elizabethan poetry and drama—this demands the original language. Unfortunately English people, probably bored by excessive exposure to their classics while at school, have up to now often neglected most of their Elizabethan heritage, except Shakespeare. In production even Shakespeare's work has only occasionally managed to avoid the pitfalls of deadening routine, operatic artificiality and intellectual whimsicality.

In order to have any influence on the younger generations Shakespearean production must renew itself with much more daring and become much more aware of the evolution taking place in the modern world of theatre and the other arts.

Such productions should be more open and frank. They should be anti-illusionary, without artificial theatricality; they should be non-operatic, non-rhetorical. A way must be found to make them convincing from the psychological point of view, exacting in their search for deep reality, of whatever kind, and, at the same time, true to their own style, maintaining the poetry which is so often forgotten.

If it is agreed that these aims express the deep, unexpressed needs of today's audiences and artists, then perhaps actors, directors and designers in the theatre might begin a search for that deep reality which can be attained only through study, understanding and appreciation of style—style considered as a reality in itself artistically bound to the expression of reality as a whole.

Open and frank, non-operatic productions imply new relationships between audiences and actor, stages which are anti-illusionary and fresh approaches to the designing of scenery, costumes and lighting. These must be in keeping with a new architecture expressive of these new conventions.

The actor, with increased responsibilities on these new stages, must develop his imaginative power as well as the strength and variety of his means of expression.

Everybody knows that the modern theatre is both threatened and enriched by commercial forms of entertainment. Photographic naturalism mixes there with realism and in the process the very notion of style is being lost.

But fortunately, in England at least, Shakespeare, in his original language, stands as a popular force with enough actuality to illuminate the modern scene; even the modern passion for "reality" can be gratified by him.

The main purpose of the Studio was therefore to conduct experiments through which a contemporary way of staging Shakespeare and the Elizabethans—and, as a consequence, other sorts of plays—could be evolved.

The work which was being done there was of crucial importance to the evolution of the English theatre. Through observing living demonstrations of style, writers had the opportunity to acquaint themselves with the means of transposition—in terms of composition, subject matter, language—which are necessary to their invention, if they are to express, not the externals, but the heart of reality. However, for Shakespeare and Stratford to have this capital impact on future generations, production and acting must possess more and more the qualities of truthfulness, of simplicity, directness and vigour, which are demanded by the young—but they must also be true in style. This is the exacting requirement of our time.

EDITOR'S NOTE

After Michel Saint-Denis' and Peter Hall's departure as Directors of the Royal Shakespeare Company, Trevor Nunn was appointed its Artistic Director. The Studio continued its work under his guidance and expanded its activities to include tours and workshops.

Chapter Three

GUIDING PRINCIPLES: THE PROGRESSION OF THE TRAINING

The training is not a step by step progress along one line of development; rather than being a single line, it is like a rope with several strands all separate but all somehow entwined to make one.

GEORGE DEVINE

I ONCE ATTEMPTED TO outline what would to me be an ideal school of theatre: it would offer a course of studies as detailed and as rigorous as any other professional training, be it law, medicine, music or architecture; a training so demanding that only study entirely devoted to it over several years could form the kind of accomplished actor needed for today's theatre.

Such training is different from most other professional training in that the instrument of the training is the human being itself—the body and soul of the actor—and that the work is done from the inside out rather than from the outside in. An actor has to be trained in a variety of disciplines, each vital in itself and intimately related to all the others.

Although a school offering such training should have a certain flexibility, the school's *basis* should be a unified programme of training. Too much teaching by trial and error is a great waste of effort for both teachers and students, and in addition to being disconcerting, especially in the early part of the training, it can prevent the laying of a solid base for the young actor.

Therefore, a more or less systematic basic plan, with some flexibility in the way of proceeding, is absolutely necessary.

This may sound contradictory, but I hope to explain why it is not. It is important to understand that what follows is not a method or a system, but a *way to work.*

The Kind of Actor We Want to Train

It is essential to make clear from the outset what kind of actor we want to develop and what sort of theatre we want to train him for.

Nowadays society and the theatre are changing so fast we cannot be sure of anything; all the more reason for the training to have a compehensive basis in all disciplines so that a complete freedom of technique, a freedom of expression and a flow of imagination can be achieved.

The question, however, is, how are we going to train the young acting student so as to prepare him to be discriminating when confronted with a multitude of outside influences and tendencies? Are we going to defend him against them or prepare him to face them?

Our conviction is that whatever experiments may be attempted, through fresh forms of writing, or on new stages—in the round, octagonal or thrust, on stages with the latest, the most advanced, technical devices, or just on bare, exposed boards — everything ultimately depends on the human being, the *actor.*

We have, therefore, to form an actor equipped with all possible means of dramatic expression, one capable of facing up to any challenge and meeting the demands of today's and tomorrow's ever-changing theatre, an actor who is capable of participating in these changes and who is himself inventive enough to contribute to them.

The Training

I have a tremendous suspicion of *any* "method," whether old or new, which stops questions or discourages change. We search for truth—but truth is always changing as our lives change.

I have planned in my time five schools, each of them aimed at establishing a complete theatrical organization, with, at its centre, a permanent, professional repertory company.

To me, such a school would combat all sorts of academic rigidity. It would dedicate itself to a renewal of acting techniques and gradually invent new ways of working, while along the way training its own teachers. Regularly—in fact at the end of every school year—it would re-examine its ways of working.

In each of the schools it was hoped that the students would develop a unified way of acting which would then become that of its repertory company.

As we consider these goals and ways of working, several factors emerge: it is of prime importance to establish from the beginning the idea of ensemble acting because what, in fact, creates life on the stage is the actor's awareness of his relationships — spiritual, imaginative, perceptive, physical — with other actors.

However, the training of the actor has to be, in its details, adapted to each individual. This is of vital importance.

The quality and standards of the school can only be ensured by continuity in the faculty and teaching. In order to arrive at a unified way of acting it is necessary to establish a unity of training, with the different branches coordinated and growing organically.

Each entering group of acting students should gradually be formed into a kind of company, which should be maintained during the entire four years of the training, if possible.

Finally, in contrast to the detailed individual exercises practiced in other branches of the training, the interpretive work should always be done by studying a whole play, or, at least, one act of a play; we must avoid the customary practice of working on isolated scenes. By continually rehearsing scenes detached from their contexts, the student takes the risk of placing too much importance on his own work instead of maintaining the necessary balance of relationships with the other characters in a play.

When I use the word actor, I actually have two sorts in mind: the kind who works with a text and the kind who works without one. When his work is based on a text, I think of him as the actor/interpreter; when he acts without a text, I call him the actor/improviser. Naturally, at the highest levels of our art these two breeds of actor tend to merge; however, for now the above distinctions will be helpful.

In most companies the actor will be placed, more often than not, in the position of interpreter: as such he finds himself confronted with a text. Having penetrated to the heart of the play, he must interpret its meaning. To do this it is necessary, above all, to submit himself to the play and this demands an objective attitude.

The truthfulness of a given text cannot be found unless an objective consideration of the nature of the text takes place at the precise moment when the actor's subjective, inner truth starts to emerge.

The connection between the subjective and the objective, the absolute necessity of constant exchanges between these two attitudes, conditions the entire progression of the work. It is through the experience of this connection, this exchange, that the interpreter, having started from his instinctive way of working, gives himself the chance to go beyond himself. Through this he can raise his imagination to the level of the most demanding texts instead of remaining miserably dependent on his own subjective identity, however profound it may be.

Yet, ultimately, in order to bring life to a part, the actor will have to move from his objective attitude to a concentration on himself. It is only from within himself, and through physical actions inspired by or drawn from his own inner resources, that the character can be realized, can finally be born. This requires a subjective attitude. From the conflict and reconciliation of these two attitudes, one can gradually obtain an interpretation which will be both faithful to the text and vitally alive.

The actor who works without receiving his initial impulse from an author, without the support of a text and without the subsequent restrictions of his obligations to it, is not an interpreter. He has been called many things at different times and in different countries: a farceur, a clown, a music-hall or vaudeville entertainer. This kind of actor is his own author, but it is rare that he actually sits down to write. He invents his text in action, as it were, on his feet—he is an improviser. In fact, he usually has no ambition to devise a work of art, he merely makes a plan which he calls a scenario or a sketch. He is directly creative.

If we accept this distinction between the actor/interpreter and the actor/improviser, should we not stimulate the initiative and invention of the future interpreter by making him pass through the experiences of the actor/creator?

Improvisation

A recognition of the value of this way of working leads us to improvisation, in all its forms, as an essential basis for the training of the actor, regardless of the kind of theatre for which he is destined. Improvisation is the way to liberate and stimulate invention; it is a fundamental way of working that opens up new and unexpected horizons for the student.

We have, of course, to define in what way we are going to use this improvisation so that it can lead to the interpretation of all styles without exception, regardless of their origin and period. We want to give interpretation a *reality* which is meaningful for our own time. I realise that here one is confronted with a very complex problem: not to confuse *reality* with *realism*. But how, and by what means, are we to help young actors—who are plunged daily into the realism of films and television, not to mention the theatre—to understand, to develop a feeling for and to invest with equal reality a character from the drama of ancient Greece, of the Spanish Golden Age or of Shakespeare? Our training should, to a certain degree, encourage in our student a passion for what is called truth. But how can we discourage the misconception that a conflict exists between this contemporary demand for truth and those lyrical, heroic, eloquent masterpieces of the past which reveal the ways of feeling and the modes of living of classical times?

To give life to a style of the past demands that the interpreter find a balance between contemporary subjective truth and the objective qualities which the text brings to him. The inner truth of the actor must unite with a truthfulness of expression: if either remains separate from the other, there is falseness and deceit.

The challenge is two-fold: how to bring the actor's need for truth gradually up to the level of the finest classical texts, and how to prevent this need for truth from clashing with the remoteness and the unfamiliarity of the *form* of these texts.

There is, of course, a preliminary problem which is unavoidable: the difficulty of understanding different cultures. Acting of our sort needs nourishment. This will be found, in part, in an appreciation of the arts and in an imaginative study of the history, religion and the social life of the historical periods which are related to the great dramatic styles. An intimate knowledge of poetry and a regular practice with various sorts of texts is also necessary. Familiarity with them is a fundamental and indispensable aid to interpretation, and can only be obtained by continuous practice.

In order to be free, the actor needs to feel himself rich, rich in resources. Abundant means of expression, derived from a study of many techniques, can produce in our actors a flexibility which will not be contradictory to their need-for-truth, but will develop the range of their creative freedom. We want these techniques to be the servants of the imagination, invisible in their execution, but very solidly established by the training.

Acting which is too set, too obvious in intention, too heavy in execution, kills truth and pleasure. The teacher/director should not force anything on the student/actor. But he must induce the student to use varied means of expression and keep his imagination always well oriented and open. Under these conditions freedom can thrive. In order to arrive at *la vie scenique*, the total life of a play on the stage, achievement of this freedom is of first importance.

There are certain elements which make this freedom possible:

- The development, at the very heart of the school and of the company, of a human and artistic milieu, which, because of its invisible pull on everyone, quite naturally breeds a climate where the quality of the professional training, the adherence to the guiding principles, the multiplicity of critical and theoretical exchanges, will spread a sense of individual responsibility, which will ultimately merge with the school's sense of ensemble. I believe that this milieu, this climate, if it is authentic and generous, could impress students and actors more profoundly than the study of even the most advanced techniques.

- The encouraging of all the artists working within such a school to advance their own views while, at the same time, directing their efforts towards a common goal—the achievement of vital work in a contemporary spirit.

- The provision of an open stage, one without the "fourth wall" and, therefore, without a proscenium. Such a stage presents a large acting area served by many different entrances. This sort of acting area makes the audience aware of the three dimensions of space and invites the actor to play *physically*; its proximity to the audience enables the actor to act truthfully without having to force his voice or enlarge his gestures.

These then are the guiding principles upon which the training is founded. In the chapters that follow each discipline is examined in detail. The emphasis throughout is on helping each student to discover the potential of his instrument—his body and his voice—and to liberate his imagination.

It seems to me vital to train, simultaneously, from the beginning, the mind, the technique and the spirit of the actor to serve the imagination.

It is also important to encourage first the dramatic instinct in the actor and through it develop invention and spontaneity. This *must* precede the work on interpretation, which is, of course, the culmination of all our effort.

A constant interrelationship of the three disciplines — movement, voice and speech — must be established very early on in the training. The student will discover how each serves the other and how the integration of all these elements makes for a strong overall impact.

If the student is not absolutely free in body and voice, that is, if he is not relaxed in the right way, he will soon discover that it will have an adverse effect on his speech and on the control of his breathing and will also disturb the rhythm and the scansion of the text.

In the first year great emphasis should be placed on the non-verbal aspects of the voice and speech training. When the student has learned, through various ways, to focus on expression without using a text, then he will be able to begin to *act* with a text.

To the student who tries to express something too early without having yet the means to do so clearly, I often say: "Do not put on a cloak and then try to dress underneath it."

Once during a lecture I was asked: "What is the most vital aspect of your training?" There is no *most* vital aspect. There is, rather, a balance between the technique on which the actor bases his activity and what is generally called the "inspiration of the actor."

Students often feel that technique hampers spontaneity, that it kills creativity. But if one has learned and absorbed technique, it becomes second nature. One is not conscious of it, but it is there—the Third Eye, the actor's ever-present unconscious control.

The Training Schedule

The training, consisting of twelve terms, three terms to a year, lasts four years. Each year of the training has been given a name which defines our principle aim for that year.

I. The Discovery Year

In this first year the student discovers what talents—physical, vocal and imaginative—nature has given him. He finds out what he has to do to develop them and to acquire technique and skills. He begins to be aware of potentialities and possibilities.

II. The Transformation Year

In his second year the student begins to learn how to use these possibilities as he acquires some knowledge of physical, vocal, and imaginative expression. As he develops these faculties, he is transformed and learns *how* to transform—that is to say, he learns how not always to be himself.

This second year has always been known as a difficult year. This is partly due to the fact that, beginning to be aware of "technique," the student feels that technique is disturbing the flow of his imaginative powers. But it is also due to the fact that we demand of the student his complete imaginative involvement. This is absolutely vital for the kind of training we propose.

III. The Interpretation Year

In this year the student, having discovered the natural equipment at his disposal and having enlarged it to some degree, acquires a certain confidence that he can now apply to the interpretation of plays in many different styles—classical and modern—and he begins to be able to project and to communicate with an audience.

IV. The Performing Year

The main activity in the fourth year is rehearsing and performing many different plays on stages as varied as possible before many kinds of audiences.

The twelfth term—at the end of the student's four years of training—should be crowned by a two-week repertory season in the school's theatre, where the student can be seen by audiences and agents. Three plays should be presented—a tragedy, a comedy and a realist play—plus an experimental piece specially devised for the group. The last could be either a musical show or an entertainment with masks, tumbling, fighting, singing and dancing, which would show the versatility of the student.

The charts provided here give details of the various branches of the training and codify our guiding principles.

FIRST YEAR, FALL TERM: DISCOVERY YEAR

TECHNIQUE			IMAGINATION		
BODY	VOICE/DICTION	SPEECH/LANGUAGE	IMPROVISATION	INTERPRETATION	IMAG. BKGD./MISC.
Emphasise full awareness of body. Just as a musician has complete control of his instrument, an actor must have coordinated control of his body. Focus on releasing tension through relaxation and developing muscular strength and flexibility. *Dramatic Movement:* Stress what different parts of the body can express. Practice "isolating" each part. Add work in Alexander Technique.	*Voice:* Develop awareness of one's physical equipment: • Organs of speech • Breathing mechanism • Resonators Find (gradually) natural pitch of each student's voice. Begin to work for "size." Do *not* yet work for projection. *Diction:* Work on purity of vowels, consonants. *Singing:* Begin singing classes after 3rd week of term.	Begin with Non-Dramatic Readings. Read simple texts of all kinds, to gain a sense of freedom and pleasure in language and to obtain *speech vitality.* Stress learning how to listen and the pure enjoyment of reading aloud to others. No demands yet on technique. This course spreads over this term and is periodically taken up later.	During the entire first year, emphasise non-verbal improvisation: • Discovering the nature of *acting.* • Learning to express action without words. • Realising what the body can express and how. Train students to observe themselves and others. Improvise using activities of everyday life. Develop initiative, invention and a sense of disciplined freedom in the student.	*The Discovery Play Project.* Students learn to act through process of rehearsals. First play's aim is to make students realise why they need training and for faculty to discover students' potentials and needs (4 weeks, 3 hours/day). The teacher / director should guide rather than direct. The project is shown to the faculty. No visitors allowed.	Criticism of the Discovery Play Project. Possibly short sessions with director to allow students to put criticism into effect. Continue all technical classes throughout the term, gradually increasing time alloted to improvisation. Schedule talks on history of stage, development of acting spaces; draw student's attention to different acting spaces and how they can affect his acting.

FIRST YEAR, WINTER TERM: DISCOVERY YEAR

TECHNIQUE			IMAGINATION		
BODY	VOICE/DICTION	SPEECH/LANGUAGE	IMPROVISATION	INTERPRETATION	IMAG. BKGD./MISC.
Continue general training, emphasising: • Sloppy relaxation and movement ↑ no expression. • Tense movement ↑ no expression. • Controlled *free* movement ↑ a current of liveliness, expressiveness, running through the body. Choose exercises that reveal differences between space, time, rhythm in real life and on the stage. Continue work with Alexander Technique.	*Voice:* Continue training. Aim at improving quality of tone. *Diction:* Practice inflections. *Singing:* Work from speech to singing, from singing to speech. Increase student's awareness of need for vocal imagination (thoughts and feelings behind words). Show how images provoke different tones or tempos when speaking.	Continue Non-Dramatic Readings. Texts chosen should be selected with regard for their style. Explore meaning. Examine value of single words. Aim at more subtlety of tone. Stop Non-Dramatic Readings after 2 weeks to make way for Play Readings.	Work on • *Location.* • *Moods.* • *Occupations.* Plan movements, then scenario, add location and mood. • *Transformations.* For the first time the student will consciously "become" someone other than himself. He will have to change physically. • *Animals.* Select animals which best capture the temperament and *essence* of the animal. • *See progression in chap. six.*	Begin readings of 3 plays in 3 different styles. Read in quick succession (2–2½ weeks each). Rehearse the last play read in a relaxed way, not pushing students to act. They are not ready. Teach them placing. Make few demands on technique or character development. At the end of the term, the project is shown to the faculty and later discussed.	Schedule talks on History of Drama throughout the first year until all major historical periods are covered. Schedule talks on costumes, customs, manners, focused on whatever period the current rehearsal project is concerned with. These talks are directly related to the student's rehearsal work; they are not theoretical courses.

FIRST YEAR, SPRING TERM: DISCOVERY YEAR

TECHNIQUE			IMAGINATION		
BODY	VOICE/DICTION	SPEECH/LANGUAGE	IMPROVISATION	INTERPRETATION	IMAG. BKGD./MISC.
Continue general body training.	Continue general training.	*L'Expression Parlée:* Establish a plan of texts, growing progressively more demand-	Continue work on transformations. Add *Group Im- provisations*, be-	Rehearse the third play (one like Obey's *Noah* or Capek's *Insect	Present pictorial documentation. Introduce practi- cal exercises that
Continue work in Alexander Tech- nique, holding sessions with in- dividuals when needed.	*Voice:* Emphasise pace, power, modula- tion, rhythm.	ing. Work inten- sively on poetry and on great speeches from classical texts. No	ginning with 2 people, then 3, then with larger groups. *The mask,* a separate course, goes on until the	*Play)* which can be related to work in mask class and in improvisation. Begin to use some of the techniques	teach students to use the styles pre- sented. Faculty and stu- dents discuss and evaluate first
Introduce ele- ments of acrobat- ics.	*Diction:* Correct faulty ac- cents.	dialogues yet. Emphasis on speaking rather than acting or character devel-	end of this term, using the basic masks. At the close of the term, Mask and Group	being acquired. Except for a few absolutely neces- sary elements, no costumes or sets	year's work.
	Singing: Stress flexibility and agility.	opment. No "di- rection" given. Also emphasise projection, style,	Improvisation work is shown to faculty.	are used. Public is not invited to showing.	
	Voice/Diction/ Singing: Later in term, be- gin to stress pro- jection.	length of breath.			

SECOND YEAR, FALL TERM: TRANSFORMATION YEAR

TECHNIQUE		IMAGINATION		
BODY	VOICE/DICTION	SPEECH/LANGUAGE	IMPROVISATION	INTERPRETATION	IMAG. BKGD./MISC.
Continue movement classes with a new teacher. Make class more demanding. Aim at generating energy and stamina. Introduce stage combat training (unarmed). Continue with Alexander Technique (individual sessions when needed).	*Voice, Diction, Singing:* Continue general training, plus correction of individual defects. Work on accents and rhythms. Emphasise • Strength of projection. • Muscular ease and relaxation. Emphasise breath control in long phrases. Consider size of diction. Plan special singing exercises to sustain long breath.	Continue work on speech and poetry. Practice sustaining breath through a long text. In poetry sessions, develop lyrical expression to its peak during this and the next terms. Practice projection of speech without effort. Emphasise necessity of vitality, in both technique and imagination. Develop sensitivity to the inner life and rhythms of a text.	Continue improvisation exercises. Review basic mask work from first year, spring term, then begin character and comic mask work. At the end of this term, arrange showings of: • a scenario with character masks. • a scenario using improvisation.	Begin rehearsal of the fourth play—a realist play. Conclude with a showing to faculty and then hold critique sessions. Later in term, start rehearsals of a Shakespeare play (e.g., *Romeo and Juliet*).	Introduce classes in makeup. Present guest lecturers who give talks on theatre in different parts of the world.

SECOND YEAR, WINTER TERM: TRANSFORMATION YEAR

	TECHNIQUE				IMAGINATION	
BODY	VOICE/DICTION	SPEECH/LANGUAGE	IMPROVISATION	INTERPRETATION	IMAG. BKGD./MISC.
Continue classes in movement (1½ hours, 3 times/ week). Build energy and stamina. Work on physical concentration.	*Voice:* Continue general training and individual voice work.	*L'Expression Parlée:* Give more attention to interpretation. No acting yet. Later in term, begin to work with 2 people. Work on light classical comedy texts. Conclude with showing of Poetry work.	To prepare for work in comedy: • Emphasise use of *imaginary* props. • Use invented speech—grummelotage (but not gibberish).	Continue rehearsals of the Shakespeare play begun last term. Show play to faculty.	Performances of the Shakespeare play and the farce should be followed by sessions devoted to criticism of the work.
Develop sense of the relationships between direction and space.	*Diction:* Emphasise individual needs.	Add speech gymnastics, such as speaking against loud noises, speaking while eating or dancing.	Rehearse a scenario prepared in the improvisation class, using imaginary props.	After the Comedy Techniques class, rehearse a farce, in which student applies all experience acquired in movement, improvisation and mask classes. Develop exuberance. Show farce to the rest of the school and a few invited guests.	
Continue work in Alexander Technique.	*Singing:* Work on choral and individual singing.		Add *Comedy Techniques* course (4-5 weeks, 2 classes/ week). This leads to the rehearsing of a farce.		
	In all classes: • Strive for more agility. • Emphasise development of vocal imagination.				

SECOND YEAR, SPRING TERM: TRANSFORMATION YEAR

TECHNIQUE			IMAGINATION	
BODY	VOICE/DICTION	SPEECH/LANGUAGE	IMPROVISATION	INTERPRETATION	IMAG. BKGD./MISC.
Continue movement classes, developing lightness and swiftness now as well as energy and stamina, so that students see the difference. Work on elevation. Continue Alexander Technique, scheduling both group and individual sessions.	Continue general training. Work on projection. Later in the term, work on colour, pitch, tempo, phrasing and the value of words. Expand development of vocal imagination by devising exercises which demonstrate how sounds relate to the senses—increase the student's perception of the functioning of the senses so that this awareness will enliven his use of words.	Continue work on l'Expression Parlée. With individual students, concentrate on poems and on speeches from the great plays of world literature. Goal now is to prepare students to cope with demands of tragedy. Stop classes for last 2-3 weeks to allow more time for rehearsal project. Resume work on l'Expression Parlée in the 3rd year.	Rehearse 1 or 2 short contrasting scenarios, invented by students, guided by teacher. These should be seen by faculty. Stop before last 3 weeks to give more time to the rehearsal project in progress.	A Russian play, one by Chekhov or in similar style, is chosen deliberately at this moment of the training because of the humanity of this sort of play. In rehearsals (6 weeks), begin to work in depth. Use scenery, furniture, costumes, props. Show play to an audience of faculty, students and some invited friends. No general public yet.	Continue makeup classes. At the end of the term, review and sum up the second year's work.

THIRD YEAR, FALL TERM: INTERPRETATION YEAR

	TECHNIQUE			IMAGINATION	
BODY	VOICE/DICTION	SPEECH/LANGUAGE	IMPROVISATION	INTERPRETATION	IMAG. BKGD./MISC.
Continue movement classes, exposing student to yet another teacher. Create more imaginative movement by emphasising the relationships between words and movement.	*Voice:* Work on exercises that enlarge projection: go from whispering to shouting and back to whispering.	Resume work in l'Expression Parlée. Aim at enlarging both the technical and emotional scale. Work on great speeches and dialogues from Shakespeare's tragedies or Greek plays. Concentrate on texts and related movement exercises that will sustain enlargement of the student's voice in preparation for the great roles in tragedy.	Cease Improvisation classes temporarily. Use this time for rehearsals. Master classes in Improvisation will begin in the fourth year.	Rehearse the seventh play, a Jacobean tragedy. Using simple scenery, costume, sound, and lights, show this tragedy to a small invited audience.	
Enlarge scale of projection. Practice projection even while remaining immobile.	*Diction:* Continue to correct accents.			The next project should be a realist play, also shown to a small invited audience.	
	Singing: Continue exercises in projection. Work on improvised singing and rhythm exercises.				
Add tap dancing.				Start yet another rehearsal project, in preparation for a short tour of schools and colleges during the winter.	
Continue work with Alexander Technique.					

THIRD YEAR, WINTER TERM: INTERPRETATION YEAR

TECHNIQUE			IMAGINATION		
BODY	VOICE/DICTION	SPEECH/LANGUAGE	IMPROVISATION	INTERPRETATION	IMAG. BKGD./MISC.
Continue last term's work (1½ hours, 3 times/ week).	*Voice-Diction:* (1 hour, 3 times/ week). Emphasise swift, clear articulation, work with short phrases.	*Speech:* To the ongoing work, add practice on dialects.	Improvisation classes are still suspended but, in middle of term, resume for 2 weeks, doing preparatory exercises in the Restoration style.	Rehearsal project continues, focused on a play, preferably a classic, suitable to be taken on tour to schools and colleges.	
Continue tap dancing twice weekly, 1½ hours).	*Singing:* Work with individuals on specific problems.	*L'Expression Parlée:* Texts should relate to the Restoration period. Exercises should be done to give practice in teasing, offering challenges, making innuendoes.		*Aims of Tour:* • To act before young audiences and to cope with their unexpected reactions.	
Continue work in Alexander Technique (teacher works mostly with individuals).	If there is a musical project planned give more time to singing classes to prepare for it.	Work with classical texts toward lightness of articulation and delivery, improved timing, increased rapidity of speech.		• To get accustomed to one-night stands. • To adapt to daily changes of acting space. After the tour, begin rehearsals for a Restoration play.	

THIRD YEAR, SPRING TERM: INTERPRETATION YEAR

TECHNIQUE			IMAGINATION		
BODY	VOICE/DICTION	SPEECH/LANGUAGE	IMPROVISATION	INTERPRETATION	IMAG. BKGD./MISC.
Carry on with movement classes (3 times/week). Maybe begin a dance-drama project: use texts that can be combined with imaginative movement (1½ hours, 3 times/week). Continue stage combat training (unarmed).	*Voice-Diction:* Continue training at an advanced level (1 hour, 3 times/week). *Singing:* Teacher works with individuals.	*Speech:* Continue training. Work on dialects. *L'Expression Parlée:* Resume work from fall term, practicing with great speeches and dialogues of world literature. Texts should become progressively more difficult. Emphasise Greek plays.	Improvisation work has been temporarily suspended.	Finish rehearsals of Restoration play. This will be the first full-fledged production, with scenery, props, lighting, costumes, sound effects. Show to rest of school and an invited audience.	Invite guest lecturers to speak on any theme related to the theatre. Have theatre managers, directors, authors, agents, theatrical lawyers discuss such topics as acting, casting, contracts, Equity, how to present auditions, etc.

FOURTH YEAR, FALL TERM: PERFORMING YEAR

	TECHNIQUE		IMAGINATION		
BODY	VOICE/DICTION	SPEECH/LANGUAGE	IMPROVISATION	INTERPRETATION	IMAG. BKGD./MISC.
Continue movement training (1½ hours, 3 times/ week). Emphasise need for energy and stamina. Teach students a series of warm-up exercises to be practiced daily. Add stage combat training (armed)—(1½ hours, 2 or 3 times/ week for several weeks). Work up to a showing in the next term.	*Voice, Diction, Singing:* Continue exercises on advanced level. Add work to "stretch" student's voice and imagination. Emphasis on tragedy: experiment with cries, as in agony, in fury, in rage, in despair, and with emotions and pauses leading to these. *Singing:* Teach students a series of warm-up exercises to be practiced daily.	*Speech:* Work mainly with individuals. Work for flexibility of emotion: students need to be "stretched" in the practice and use of the longer emotional scale, the rendering of expressions of courage, horror, revenge, hate, doom, both choral and individual as required in performing such plays as *Oedipus, Medea, Trojan Women.*	Begin master classes with special exercises at an advanced level (6 weeks). Continuing stage combat training, improvise to build up a scenario that combines armed combat with appropriate texts.	Begin Play Rehearsal Project—a Greek or a Shakespearean tragedy. Rehearsals lead to a performance in the school theatre to an invited audience (the public but no press, no agents). Begin rehearsals for the next project—a realist play.	Present guest speakers—for example, Arthur Miller, John Gielgud, Eva Le-Gallienne, Harold Clurman, Peter Hall, Zoe Caldwell, Liviu Ciulei. Continue instruction in makeup.

FOURTH YEAR, WINTER TERM: PERFORMING YEAR

	TECHNIQUE			IMAGINATION		
	BODY	VOICE/DICTION	SPEECH/LANGUAGE	IMPROVISATION	INTERPRETATION	IMAG. BKGD./MISC.
	Continue movement training (1½ hours, 3 times/ week).	*Voice:* Continue training (1 hour, 3 times/ week), with special sessions as needed.	*Speech:* Continue work with individuals. Hold special sessions as needed.	No improvisation work, unless something special is needed for the rehearsal projects for the repertory season or unless there is opportunity to offer a unique master class.	Complete the rehearsals of the realist play project started before Christmas. End with a performance for the public.	
	Dance/movement teacher prepares a project to be shown to faculty and small audience (1½ hours, 3 times/week). Continue stage combat training (armed)—(1½ hours for a period of several weeks). Then show a scenario.	*Singing:* Work with individuals. Give more time to rehearsals if a musical is planned for the repertory season.	Stretch student's capacity for vocal imagination as related to tragedy —student needs carrying power to lengthen phrases, to extend them across space without shouting.		*Repertory Season:* In preparation for the repertory season, re-rehearse the Shakespeare or Greek tragedy as well as the other previously performed plays chosen for inclusion in the repertory schedule. Do 3 to 4 plays and one experimental show.	

FOURTH YEAR, SPRING TERM: PERFORMING YEAR

TECHNIQUE			IMAGINATION		
BODY	VOICE/DICTION	SPEECH/LANGUAGE	IMPROVISATION	INTERPRETATION	IMAG. BKGD./MISC.
Continue to build energy and stamina (1 hour, 3 times/week). Experiment with more subtle movements. The rest of the time is scheduled for rehearsing the plays for the repertory season.	*Voice-Diction:* Continue training (1 hour, 3 times/week). *Singing:* Work with individuals. Keep up with rehearsals for the repertory season, working out any specific problems as necessary.	Work with individuals. Help students to prepare auditions for agents, directors, etc.	Stop (unless improvisational techniques are needed for the repertory plays). Offer a master class (perhaps one with masks).	Rehearse for the repertory season. Schedule 2 or 3 weeks of performances to take place in the school's theatre. The audience should include general public, press and agents. Supervised warm-ups for body and voice should be done before each performance.	

Chapter Four

THE ACTOR'S TECHNIQUES: PHYSICAL AND VOCAL EXPRESSION

Suit the action to the word, the word to the action.
Hamlet

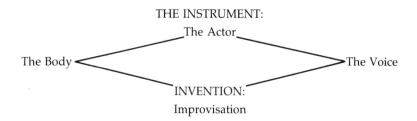

THE INSTRUMENT:
The Actor

The Body

The Voice

INVENTION:
Improvisation

Some General Considerations

TOO OFTEN IN BOOKS about training for the theatre subjects are treated from a technical point of view only. We want to avoid this because there is far more to training than technique.

These few notes preceding the description of our way of training the body and voice can be thought of as a framework on which a course of studies can be planned. They also indicate the spirit and "climate" in which the work should be done.

In Chapter Three I explained the difficulty of balancing the work between pure technique and imagination and of *not* letting technique take the first place. That place in the training should be given to work on developing the actor's imagination, the creative spirit of the actor.

In general, in each section of the training the exercises should have a dramatic justification, so that pure technique is very early on related to imagination. The student will then gradually begin to apply this concept himself without the teacher's help. Here are a few examples of some simple physical exercises with dramatic justifications.

Once a student has learned how to walk properly, he is asked:

- to walk towards a person he sees in the street and wants to greet.
- to walk in a street where he sees somebody he wants to avoid.
- to walk in the street in a meandering, aimless way.

For vocal exercises with dramatic justifications, the teacher might invent exercises in which, for instance, the student talks to different types of people:

- a tall person
- a small person
- somebody he loves
- somebody he hates
- a child or a grown-up person
- a superior or an employee

This will influence the tone of the student's voice, the rhythm of his speech and many other things.

PART I: THE BODY

> Action is the essence of theatre, and action is movement.
>
> JACQUES COPEAU

Movement is a more elementary, instinctive, direct means of expression than speech; it increases the dramatic feeling, clarifies the intention of a text and gives a precise image of it.

In acting, movement becomes the physical expression of

words and gives concrete form to the meaning of a text; it is the outer expression of the inner continuity of a role.

In life one moves for many reasons:

- as a result of physical necessity
- at the prompting of a sudden idea
- in consequence of a changing emotional state

It is difficult to "lay down the law" about how to train the actor's body and increase his range of physical expression. There are many very excellent books written about body training and I do not profess to be an expert on the *technical* approach to this question, but I *do* know what is needed for the actor. Having been an actor myself and with forty years experience in training actors, I think I am in a position to determine certain basic guidelines on this subject.

It may be helpful to be reminded that the body has three basic mechanical functions:

- stretching
- bending
- rotating

Among these three functions there are endless possibilities for interaction and interchange, all leading to richness of physical expressiveness.

The student must be taught how to isolate different muscle groups and work them at will, independently, without involving the rest of the body. To attain our aim of relaxation, flexibility and strength, the student goes through simple exercises of:

- the head
- the neck
- the shoulders
- the upper arms
- the lower arms
- the wrists
- the hands
- the fingers
- the torso

- the spine
- the centre of the body
- the hips
- the thigh
- the lower part of the leg (from the knee down)
- the ankle
- the foot
- the toes

Dramatic Movement

When the student has learned how to isolate the various parts of his body and has become aware of, has experienced, each of them and has achieved some kind of "technique," he is shown how each part of his body can express something by itself:

- Shoulders can be shrugged to express different moods: rebellion, indifference, grief.
- The head turns at a call from behind. (The student should attempt to move the head without involving the shoulders or the upper body.)
- The legs can kick at somebody or something, violently or gently.
- The foot can push something away or draw it near.
- The hands, using just the motion of the wrist, can express a state of mind.
- The hips can push a person away or, indeed, a piece of furniture.

These are only a few obvious examples. Their purpose is to make the student realise that he has to go through the whole gamut of physical exercises for one purpose only: to make *all* parts of his body expressive.

The beginner, not yet able to draw upon his finer, inner resources for outward physical expression, will probably at first use for his acting only the most obvious, mechanical, everyday gestures, such as:

- placing the hands on the hips with arms akimbo to express menace.
- expressing pleasure by a sharp taking-in of breath and opening of the mouth.

- taking a step backwards to express fear or horror.
- expressing surprise by dilating the eyes and opening the mouth.
- expressing fear by raising the arms in front of the face.

The student should be made aware, though, of many other possibilities for expressing horror, pleasure, surprise or fear.

After a time spent on the isolating exercises the student begins to put the whole body together again.

Then we go on to a variety of exercises that show the student how, as an actor, to walk, run and leap; how to stand, relaxed or tense; and, of course, how to flex and strengthen the abdominal muscles. We also work on the stretching, relaxing and tensing of all the muscle groups and the unblocking of all muscular tensions.

All this will make the student aware of the interplay between the different parts of his body and the source from which the impulse-action for this interplay springs.

The student should also learn that in whatever he does, however small the gesture he uses, a kind of current, *life*, must go through the *whole* body. He will gradually discover that his entire body takes part in the gesture even if it does not move with it.

The originating motor of movement should be in the centre of the body, from which all movement passes to the extremities, creating a continuous flow. To permit this current to flow even if one does not move, a great deal of control is needed. If the movement is done mechanically, it does not leave anything behind it; it has no more effect on an actor's expressiveness than water running through a tap.

All exercises should aim at producing a state of balanced physical well-being, a state of poised relaxation which leads to an agile control of timing.

This physical well-being is important to an actor's imaginative growth and is essential to the development of his means of expression.

This is why, at the Juilliard School, we have added the Alexander Technique to our training of the body. The Alexander Technique, invented by F. Matthias Alexander and described in his book *The Use of Self*, is a method by which the student can free himself of postural bad habits and become aware of the meeting point of his body and mind. At the same time the Technique corrects the alignment of his body and his co-ordination in general.

The student's imaginative involvement in all the foregoing work is vital. But one will often find that a student beginning to be aware of "technique" will feel that technique is disturbing the flow of his imaginative powers. It is only after the student has achieved a considerable mastery of all his expressive means that he will be able to accept technique and use it as an aid to his imagination.

It is good from time to time to end these classes with five or ten minutes of completely improvised dancing, to music or to a percussion instrument, in order for the students to release tensions, to relax and to enjoy themselves.

This sense of physical well-being and the feeling of being in control of the body that our training in movement, acrobatics, tap dancing, fencing and fighting produces helps to develop stamina in the student's nervous system and to diminish his fear of heights and falls.

There have been actors who have brilliantly overcome this almost universal fear of heights and falls: Laurence Olivier in his production of *Hamlet* at the St. James Theatre in London jumped off a platform approximately eleven feet high, somersaulted through the air and landed on the ground in front of the platform where he immediately began to engage in a fight.

Alan Badel once played a soldier in John Gielgud's production of *Macbeth*. In the heat of the battle of Dunsinane, he ran onto a platform high above the stage, stopped at its edge, turned to shoot, only to be hit himself and fall backwards off the platform, onto the stage.

These are no mean feats; they require a great deal of preparation, practice, courage and will power.

Reality in life is not reality on the stage. But the observation of life is one of our best teachers. It is important that attention be drawn to the differences between the real world and the stage world, especially with regard to

- space
- time
- rhythm

Exercises should be invented to point out these differences so that a sense of stage space, stage time and stage rhythm will be developed in the student.

Relaxation

All exercises should be done in a state of relaxed concentration. The ability to relax physically and mentally is one of the essential, basic acquisitions for an actor. The right kind of relaxation is a form of concentration; it is a condition of being *available*, of being ready to spring into action at any moment. It also is a state of receptivity and readiness for immediate communication.

The Feeling for Stage Space

In these days when a new theatre architecture is developing and there is a great variety of stages and auditoriums, it is essential for an actor to have a feeling for space, a memory for space and an ability to adapt to stages of different shapes and sizes.

It is not the same thing to act on the conventional proscenium stage—where the actors always act within the same area, facing the audience, but separated from them by a barrier of footlights and an orchestra pit—and to act in a theatre in the round, where the audience encircles the stage and sees the play from different angles at different moments: the position of the stage has changed, but there is still separation of audience and actor. This presents problems to the director, who must not only have a great feeling for space himself, but also for the moments of a play the whole audience must understand and *see.* He will therefore have to place and move his actors in subtle ways. The problems for the actor are even more difficult: if, for instance, an actor in a key moment of the play has to turn his back to one part of the audience in order to speak to another actor who is facing this same part of the audience, he must be able to vary his positions slightly from time to time and also know how to act with his back. This does not mean fussy twitchings and changing of weight from one foot to the other; it means, rather, that the actor must feel when he has to shift his position in order not to mask another actor who might, for instance, shift his rehearsed position in a moment of passion or anger.

There is a famous theatre in Mannheim, Germany, Das Kleine Haus of the National Theatre, which was built after the Second World War, where, along each side wall a runway descends towards the central stage. Action can take place on these runways simultaneously with that on the main stage. I once saw a play there in which two enemy armies came down the runways and converged on the central, main stage where a group of people was waiting for them in frozen horror. When, after the armies met and clashed, some of the characters, trying to escape by way of the runways, mingled with the oncoming armies in utter but well-planned confusion, the audience, on swivel seats, could follow the actors from any angle they wished to. This was tremendously exciting.

To stage such a play without accidents demanded well-trained actors, as most people do not have a natural, sensitive feeling for space: to prove this, one has only to watch people in a crowded shopping area constantly bumping into each other.

Space, a feeling for space, is something an actor must develop in himself—and not only in terms of distance from himself to another actor, to an exit, or to a piece of furniture.

The actor must also have a feeling for space he does not *see*. If in a tragedy an actor has to retreat slowly, silently, towards a seat behind him and if, not "feeling" the seat near, he crashes into it, tragedy is likely to turn into comedy.

Space is also something the actor must be able to create: he must have the faculty of giving, even on a cramped stage, the feeling of a vast ocean or a desert. I purposely do not say give an illusion of space, because to the actor this space *must be real*. It is not a question of learning technical tricks, but a feeling for space can, to some extent, be developed by exercises.

Then there is also what I like to call the *strength* of space: in relation to a specific text, some places on the stage are better to speak from, or have more impact on an audience, than others. There is no hard and fast rule about this—it is not that downstage has more impact than upstage or right more than left. There is a subtlety about this that cannot be easily described; it must be experienced.

Rudolf Laban, the eminent dance theoretician, devised exercises in the 1920's to accustom his pupils to move around a "point of interest," making their moves around or towards or away from a strong-point of radiation. That is to say, they had to discipline their sense of space with precision. We adopted these valuable exercises for our acting students with considerable success.

Direction in space is another factor to explore. For instance, one might think that a positive statement in a text would seem stronger when delivered with a forward or downstage move. But one may discover—surprisingly—that sometimes the same words spoken while taking steps backwards have more impact.

Distances and the timing of distances are other points to consider. Space often has to be telescoped on the stage and exercises should be devised for that purpose, such as: running onto the stage very fast, as if being pursued by somebody, suddenly stopping to look back and then starting to run again in another direction. It is not easy to learn how to control the sudden contraction of muscles needed for a dead stop.

Another matter to explore is how much space, and time, one needs in order to make an exit in proper relationship to the text, or how to determine how near one should be to an actor one has to approach during a short sentence. An exit in an explosion of fury can be completely spoiled by running short of text, when the move and text should end together with the actor disappearing offstage.

At every moment, the actor must feel that whatever he does or says is communication, and this must be a two-way communication. In the conventional theatre's relationship between stage and auditorium there is both communion and distinct separation at the same time. But this separation is only physical—the more receptive the actor is to a give-and-take with his audience, the easier he will be able to break down the physical barrier.

Summing Up

It might be useful here to come back to some points already mentioned in this chapter: the movement classes in the first year lay the groundwork for all the other branches of the training. Movement is not practiced as movement *per se*—it is initially practiced to liberate the body, which then, in turn, serves the dramatic expression and imagination in all the other classes.

In the second year more imaginative movement classes should be held and in the third year more subtle shape should be given to the student/actor's movement and gestures.

In order to establish a habit, movement should be practiced regularly throughout the whole four years.

PART II: THE VOICE

> She speaks poignards and every word stabs.
> *Much Ado About Nothing*

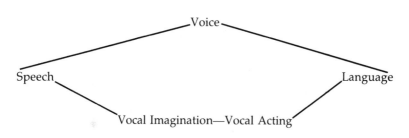

A Spoken Technique Based on Singing

Our training of the actor's voice is based on singing, in order to obtain a vocal quality in the actor that is strong, clear, rhythmic and musical. We are not speaking here of beauty or musicality for their own sake; our concern is to awaken in the actor a musical and a poetic sensitivity capable of being translated to the stage by the rhythmic quality of the voice and by modulated tones conditioned by the text. All this must start from within and find its full outer expression through the voice.

However well trained the actor's pronunciation, it is the tone, the variety of tone, in his speaking voice that has the strongest emotional and artistic impact on an audience. Artists of the radio are well aware of this.

Travelling extensively through Western and Eastern Europe we found that in countries that had deeply rooted, continuing folklore traditions, the voices, in speaking and singing, had far more variety in tone and expression and were much richer in their possibilities for use in the theatre than the voices in the so-called industrialised countries.

We want the actor to have at his disposal vocal resources that will permit him to work in all kinds of plays, whatever their form or style. It is therefore necessary for him to have a wide range of tones, a powerful voice and a breathing system he can command; there must be great flexibility and complete control of his vocal faculties.

It seems to me that this can best be obtained through the study of singing.

We were fortunate to have at the Old Vic Theatre School the great singing teacher and coach for the Glyndebourne Opera, Jani Strasser. He evolved a technique for actors, based on singing, which aimed at producing sound that was meaningful and expressive. He called singing an elaboration of speech, and his teaching technique was based on this principle. He had a great sense of theatre and acting and a way of teaching without "teaching." He taught his students breath control that seemed effortless: All his students could sing—even the tone deaf. He had them sing nonsense words and sometimes in foreign languages unknown to them, which slowly helped them to increase the articulation and clarity of their speech as well as to improve the placement of their voice.

The class would start by singing in unison, to piano accompaniment, a phrase or a verse: later the words were repeated without the melody. And then again with the melody, and so forth. Gradually the students began to speak with resonance and a variety of tones; their range increased and their breath control, so essential to good articulation, became more secure. In short, the musical quality became almost instinctive.

Most of Strasser's exercises were done with body movements which, he believed, contributed to the liberation of the voice. He would make the students swing their arms while singing or speaking. Or they would do push-ups, or lie on the floor on their backs, raising and lowering their legs while practicing breathing exercises. Sometimes they would skip around the room or run quickly in a circle. The diction teacher worked in close relationship with him and they exchanged exercises with each other.

I have seen again and again how enriching it is for actors to be taught singing not only in English but also in other languages; they greatly benefit from being able to use the unique special sounds of each language. This gives a special flexibility to the lips, tongue and other organs of speech.

Besides Jani Strasser, we had as Head of the Speech and Language Department, Marion Watson. She was in charge of supervising the relationship between the voice, speech and language teaching, and it was she who chose all the texts for the work in the school, carefully avoiding the use of great masterpieces in the technical work of the first and second years. A list of suitable texts was distributed throughout her department at the beginning of each school year. She also taught the Non-Dramatic Readings, the Play Readings and the Poetry classes and directed plays as well.

It is through such a person that the Director of a school can keep himself informed of the real progress in the various departments and can be sure that the interrelation of disciplines is maintained.

The training of the voice is the most difficult and time-consuming of all theatre disciplines. Voice formation should continue for the entire four years of the training, since, without such an extended training, it is, in most cases, quite impossible to achieve any real control. It should be stressed that the actor's vocal faculties must be continuously exercised, not only during the student's work at the school, but throughout his entire professional career. In fact, he should never stop working on his voice: the voice changes with age, whether it be a woman's or a man's voice.

One of the most illuminating remarks on this was one that Stanislavski once made when, at the age of seventy, he was about to undertake the acting of a role which was new to him: "At last I understand how to use my voice!"

Usually students (and even many practicing actors) have no idea where their voice is placed. It is for the teacher to discover this with them.

It is important, therefore, that the student have, in his first term, only one voice teacher. The reason for this is that he should not be exposed to conflicting theories at the beginning of his training; this easily happens when several teachers teach a student the same discipline in different ways at the same time.

There are, for instance, various theories about breathing, and they can be very confusing: there is chest breathing, where the resonance comes from the thorax, and abdominal breathing, which seems to be the most natural way of breathing in children. The actor should learn the uses of both and utilise them as necessary. He should be able to change easily from chest to abdominal breathing depending on the position of his body: i.e., whether he is lying down on his face, on his back, on his side with his knees drawn up to his chest, or lying "dead" on the floor facing the audience. In fact, it is useful when gathering a new faculty to arrange meetings in order to discuss what kind of breathing should be taught to begin with, and also how to unify the teaching language. The movement and dance teachers should be present at such meetings.

Until the ground work is laid and until he knows more about what he has to do, the student should be allowed to find his voice in a relaxed, but concentrated, way.

With the teacher's help, he will discover and gradually release the potential of his own vocal resources. The student's voice should be considered an individual voice, quite different from any other, and he should be encouraged to keep it so. The emphasis in the first term should be on this; any standardization of sound should be avoided.

From the very beginning, the faculty should establish a constant liaison between the body and voice classes, and go on doing so right through the successive phases of the student's development.

I am not a technician of voice or a teacher of speech, but I worked for many years with Jacques Copeau in his laboratory/school. There he made us experiment with voice and speech in various ways. This had a lasting effect on me and led me to more experiments with my own company and also in my several schools. Through these experiments I came to see the need to free speech training from its long servitude to elocution.

Having presented my qualifications as a non-specialist, I would like to say a few words about certain aspects of speech training that have occurred to me over a long life of *listening:*

Diction to me is the branch of training that helps the student towards accuracy in his use of words; it teaches him to recognise the different sounds in words, and the purity of these sounds; through the study of diction accents can be corrected and the student can become aware of the importance of articulation.

But there is a danger in misunderstanding the true meaning of diction: a student can come to pronounce words too carefully, he can begin to "elocute," giving equal length-in-time to every syllable and thereby killing all the life and rhythm of a text.

The study of diction should be started early on in the training. Clear diction and the ability to create purity of sound should be the servants of interpretation.

Rhythm is the pulsation of the text. It has an effect on the colour of speech and its meaning. The power of rhythm can be quite extraordinary in the compelling impact it can have on an audience.

There should be specific exercises on rhythm, such as:

- Rhythmic exercises with the body to make the student aware of physical rhythms.
- Rhythmic exercises with sounds only (but no words).
- Then rhythmic exercises combining movement *and* sound.
- Rhythmic exercises with words only; then with phrases leading progressively to carefully selected speeches or poetry that has marked rhythms and pronounced changes of rhythms.
- Some rhythm exercises could be based on words and changes

of moods, expressed physically first, then with short passages from texts appropriate to those moods, then, finally, combining the two.

As one will see these exercises belong to different branches of training: some to the movement class, some to the improvisation class, some to speech classes. But I list them here together for three distinct reasons. *First,* the heads of the different departments should work in close collaboration in order to devise the right kind of exercises and also to avoid any overlapping of the exercises they invent. *Second,* they should also invent combined exercises as mentioned above. *Third,* and this is the most important reason of all, there should be a short, intense period of time devoted to rhythm in all departments, not forgetting the Non-Dramatic-Readings class, where specially selected texts, with marked changes of rhythms, could be read at this time.

This would become a veritable onslaught going through the whole school, thus bringing home to the student most vividly the vital importance of rhythm.

The rhythm onslaught might best happen sometime toward the end of the first term or early in the second. It is a useful way to break the routines of classes and bring in a breath of fresh air. It is also a good way to attract the student's attention to specific subjects.

These onslaughts should not be organised by adding extra classes to the schedule, nor should they necessarily mean rescheduling: we simply replace a few classes with this special activity.

This way of planning the work obliges the faculty to collaborate more closely with each other with the result that they, too, refresh themselves.

Modulation exercises must also be practiced in detail while training the voice and the ear. For an actor to have emotional power, he must find a tone and intensity which fits the text and is not willfully superimposed on it. It is, therefore, very important to practice short passages of texts which bring this home strongly. Great attention should be given to establishing a relationship between thought, feeling and speed. In learning how to modulate the voice, the student, following a given feeling indicated in a text, plays with the voice in order to translate this feeling melodiously, but in a direct way, into the right kind of sound.

Here are some exercises which can be used to develop a sensitivity in the ear to changes of tone:

- Choose a mood or feeling, and, without using a text, find the right tone for that feeling. This should be done *not* with words, but with sounds and exclamations.
- After that, using words, select phrases that demand changes of tone and pace and relate those phrases to changes in feeling by means of modulating the tone, its intensity, etc.
- It is also useful to work on several consecutive phrases where a change of tone is necessary from phrase to phrase and, consequently, the feeling of the next phrase has to be prepared slightly in advance.

For the purpose of these exercises it is best to make up phrases rather than to use existing texts. This is done so as not to "fatigue" a text the student may one day be called upon to act.

These exercises should at first be done without any attempt at physical expression, so that the student's attention can be entirely on his vocal acting. This is very important, as otherwise physical acting will predominate and the concentration on vocal acting will disappear.

In this series of exercises, as in most others I have described, every sound the student projects must have its imaginative roots.

Vocal Imagination

As we use improvisation in the training of an actor to develop the *physical* imagination needed to arrive at physical acting, just so we should develop in the actor the *vocal* imagination needed to arrive at vocal "acting." From the fusion of these two elements, the total actor of today will emerge.

In the early part of the training, the discipline of physical acting—in improvisation—and the discipline of vocal acting—in the voice and speech classes—run separately, but parallel. Gradually, they join and become one.

I cannot stress enough the importance of developing vocal imagination. This should be accomplished through exercises that aim at spontaneous vocal, but *non-verbal*, reactions to feelings, moods, and provocations. These are devised as an antidote to the exercises in pure technique. Students often become somewhat inhibited by being made too conscious of technique. These exercises help to break down those inhibitions without neglecting pure technique. There should be a continuous flow and exchange between vocal technique and vocal imagination.

I don't think it is an exaggeration to say that speech has become more and more mechanical. Many people, and particularly the visually-educated young people of today, speak without really relating thought and feeling to words and their real meaning. Speech has also become separated from the senses, from the body, but the senses and the body cannot be so separated and an awareness of this affinity should be developed before any demands are made on the student's use of words. The awareness, the perception of the functioning of the senses has become blunted and therefore does not produce the chemistry that leads to vitality of speech and communication.

As in improvisation, where we dispense with texts to discover physical acting, one should dispense with words to discover vocal acting.

If we dispense at first with words, it is only to make clear that words are the *result* of an inner state, an inner, physical state, related to the senses, which conditions the spoken word.

So the first exercises should aim at making the student's voice expressive without using words.

This can be done by using sounds only, sounds to interpret various moods, feelings or states of mind. These sounds could, for instance, include humming sounds, or clicking sounds done with the tongue. The Italians use clicking sounds that can express regret, disapproval, anger, etc. In French we have an expression, "oh-la-la," that, said in different tones, can express many different things.

Other sound exercises could be based on sounds of the elements or the noises of nature: rain, wind, storms, the sea, waves, water lapping against the side of a boat, wind rustling through a cornfield. Or one might use the sounds of birds or other animal noises of any kind.

This non-verbal aspect of the vocal training of the beginning acting student is, to me, an utter necessity.

One should then begin to use one- or two-syllable words, like "yes" or "no" or "never," and invent exercises that use these words in a great variety of tones; this could be done in a series of questions and answers, the answer being "yes" or "no" said in different tones, according to the mood or feeling. In the one-woman play by Cocteau, *The Telephone,* we hear the actress using "yes" or "no" many times and it should be clear from the tone what she feels in reaction to the person who speaks to her on the other end of the telephone, whose voice we do not hear. (Students would benefit from listening to Liv Ullman's recording of this play.)

From here one could go on to exercises with longer words, then to phrases.

One could also experiment by repeating longer passages, using different tones and changes of rhythm and pace in order to draw the student's attention to how meaning can be distorted or completely changed by these variations.

During the early period there should be breathing exercises related to individual sounds, then isolated words and, finally, whole sentences.

Another very good exercise is to choose phrases from poems, plays, prose, folk songs or pop songs which could be practiced in different moods. Or let the student do the following exercise: begin by silently thinking a phrase, then whispering it, speaking it and, finally, singing it; then back again to speaking, whispering, thinking. A follow-up of this exercise could be gliding from speaking to singing and gliding back to speaking. In all this the changes in the breathing process should be carefully observed.

There is one more aspect of the training I would like to discuss: it is the two-way communication between the actor and the audience, the speaker and the listener. This communication can only happen if the actor conveys clearly the meaning of what he is saying and the kind of emotion he is feeling; he must be heard and "read" by the listeners—not only the audience but also the other actors. The speaker must know how to project. This is not a question of volume; it is possible for a whisper to be heard even in a large theatre. But no matter how well trained the speaker is, the hearers must have the ability to listen perceptively.

This then leads us to two things:

- One must learn how to listen to silence. This applies equally to a speaker as well as to a listener. Nowadays, when background noise is, alas, part of our lives and blunts perceptive hearing and appreciation of the finer points of *what* we hear, it is vital to make the student aware of the importance of silence, as well as of sound.
- One must learn how to *project* sound, and how to measure sound-distances.

This question of projection is a difficult one. An exercise that often proves very helpful is to put a large gong on a stand and speak at it so that the gong begins to vibrate. One can experiment with different qualities of tone, spoken from different distances, and listen to the variations in sound which are produced.

A variation on this exercise in projection is for the speaker to stand near a wall and speak at it; then to repeat the exercise at gradually greater distances from it. In spite of altering the distance, the voice should "hit" the wall with the same strength each time. Surprisingly enough, one will be aware whether or not this has been accomplished.

A good actor must know how to vary volume and projection. He will find it very helpful if he can judge for himself how much projection is needed for theatres of various sizes and shapes.

The direction in which an actor speaks is another factor to take into account: few student/actors adjust the volume of their voices when they turn upstage or speak to somebody offstage.

The student should also know how to adjust his voice to indicate whether he is speaking out-of-doors or indoors. On today's stages, where there is often no decor to define stage-space, much is indicated by the actor's body in space and by the tone of his voice.

There is a whole area in the training which we call Speech

Gymnastics where the student has to deal with such obstacles as speaking through laughter or while eating an apple, speaking against stage-effects or a storm or battle noises, speaking while dancing a lively dance or while running off the stage.

A student who has gone through the training process described above will use words and language in a fresh, liberated way; he will be able to reach his listener's ear, his mind and his senses.

Such exercises are continued throughout the first and second terms with the aim of extending the liberating process we have applied earlier to the teaching of voice-speech-language.

This work runs parallel to a new departure in the training which we introduce towards the middle of the first term.

THE PRACTICE OF TEXTS

Actors in their professional life will often be presented with a text or a play which is not in itself exciting; it is up to the actor to make that text or play stimulating enough to catch the audience's attention.

Non-Dramatic Readings

The purpose of beginning with some Non-Dramatic Readings is to develop in the student the ability to bring to life non-dramatic texts and enable him to discover the pleasure of reading aloud to others. Texts of all kinds can be used: current magazines, reports of court cases or accidents, short passages from the Bible, nursery rhymes, or even recipes from cook-books. These texts should not be too colourful or interesting in themselves; it is up to the student to make them interesting. *What* he reads is not as important as *how* he reads it. To do this convincingly he must learn to recognise the nature of the text and the intention of the writer.

In the beginning little demand should be made on the student; his technical deficiencies in diction, phrasing and inflection should be overlooked, so that he gains a sense of freedom by finding pleasure in language and, above all, feels the enjoyment of reading to others. The chief emphasis here should be on speech and communication.

This work should be informal and a relaxed feeling should be established between the teacher and student.

In the beginning the student can choose to read seated, standing or walking about; but never while slouching. The only way the student can make these readings come alive is to let a current flow from the words through his whole being; this will, consequently, transmit itself to the listener. The student is not asked to *act* in any way—the emphasis is on speaking. He should not worry about technical deficiencies, but he will no doubt be aware of them, because in his voice and speech classes attention will have been drawn to them. His whole attention here must be given to liberating his speaking.

The work on the Practice of Texts is often hard for a beginning student, because he is anxious to move on and *act*. It will take some time for him to understand why he has to do these readings; but it is not very useful to explain why: let him go through the experience a number of times before even attempting to talk about it.

It might be useful for the teacher to vary the approach to these classes. From time to time the student should be asked to improvise actions when a piece lends itself to this; or he could relate an event in his own words and then re-enact it silently; or he might invent a story of his own. In this way he will begin to relate his speaking to "doing."

One might ask a student to read a newspaper report of a crime in an objective, uninvolved way. Then ask him, or another student, to read the report again, but to read it as if he were actually seeing the crime happening. By comparing these two contrasting readings, the teacher can help the class evaluate the impact of different ways of reading.

It is naturally important to choose the right kind of text for such variations.

Once we have succeeded in establishing in the student a relaxed way of reading, in liberating his speech and helping him to find joy in tasting words, we can begin, gradually, to draw his attention to breathing, projection, and, particularly, to phrasing. We can now begin to make the student aware of the necessity of breath-control and the problems involved in phrasing short sentences as well as longer paragraphs. It should be pointed out that breath is often taken to indicate a change in feeling; with these changes the breath grows bigger or smaller or is modified in other ways. This leads the student almost automatically to an understanding of the relationship between meaning and inflection, tone, pace and rhythm. Great care should be taken not to make this phase of the work intellectual; that is to say, we must not make the student think or analyse, but, rather, sense, feel, experience.

All this should not be done in a spirit of correction—the student should still be encouraged to feel free and not be made self-conscious—he should, rather, be guided by the teacher to discover for himself his own defects and understand what, specifically, he has to work for.

We now move on to more difficult texts, texts with some literary value. While they are of increasing complexity and higher quality, they are still of a non-theatrical nature in order, once again, not to expose the student to the temptation to act before he is ready. By this time he will have acquired some knowledge of his own instrument—his body, his voice, his breathing—and, above all, the possibilities of language. One might almost say he has acquired an ability to "play" with his voice.

The student is now ready for us to make more demands on him. Having established in him a sense of pleasure, of joy in his work on a wide variety of texts, we are now in no danger of limiting his spontaneity when we bring technical matters to his attention. And yet, the emphasis at this time is still on the meaning and colour of words. Our aim is to show the student how he can feel words in a more sensuous way, how he can use language instinctively rather than intellectually.

He is now secure enough for us to comment on his work and criticise his ability to transmit the flavour of a piece; we can begin to point out, even in the simplest texts, the relationship between form and meaning. Thus, without the student necessarily being aware of it, he has taken the first steps toward an understanding of the notion of style. He will gradually begin to appreciate language, to discover the texture of language and to distinguish between different styles of writing.

During the second term the work on the Practice of Texts continues. The texts chosen for this phase should be of a more advanced kind and should be selected with a conscious regard for their style.

We should try to give the student a sense of the different ways in which words may be used and try to make him aware how language changes in different periods. He should also be helped to come to understand and differentiate in a broad and general way, the various characteristics of a piece of writing: is the piece comic, tragic, satirical or ironical, is it narrative, intimate, formal, casual, didactic or declamatory.

Works of contrasting style should be read aloud in the same session so that their forms can be compared. For example, an early seventeenth century description of the breaking up of the ice in the River Thames from *The Diary of John Evelyn* (1684) is set side by side with Virginia Woolf's twentieth century treatment of the same subject in *Orlando*.

Several classes should be devoted to speeches, such as Queen Elizabeth I's speech to the fleet at Tilbury, Churchill's speech in June 1940 "We shall fight them on the beaches. . .," Lincoln's address at Gettysburg, Roosevelt's Second Inaugural Address, Hitler's Anschluss Declaration or Edward VIII's abdication statement. Personal letters from various periods in the past also have their place in this work.

To complement these exercises on texts and to increase the actor's imaginative background, it is essential to encourage the student to do a certain amount of general reading on his own. He should be given a list of masterpieces of the great novelists of the world, chosen for their dramatic character. Around these readings general discussions should be held—not merely to insure that the reading has been done, but because it can be extremely valuable to discuss with the students some of the characters they are reading about. Certainly acquaintance with characters in the works of Dostoievski, Tolstoy, Balzac, Stendhal, Dickens, Edgar Allan Poe and Henry James, or of characters brought to life by such contemporary writers as Graham Greene and Albert Camus, can add an imaginative range to the student's experience which may, surprisingly, be more valuable in his creative work than his memory of people encountered in his own life.

It is also helpful to ask the students to choose selections on their own; from this one can often learn a great deal about a student's imagination and his progress.

Another purpose of these readings is to give the student a general introduction to the wide range of styles which exists in prose and poetry, in theatrical and non-theatrical writing. All of these are part of his national and international heritage.

As the style of the prose texts becomes more defined, the student will gradually become more aware of the nature and importance of form and of the need to respect it. Texts, at this stage, should be selected to emphasize this point. The student should be capable of understanding and dealing with form's relationship to meaning by the time Non-Dramatic Readings are superseded by work in poetry.

It should also be pointed out to the student that although in the Non-Dramatic Readings they have a certain freedom, as soon as they encounter form in texts, be it poetic or of any other kind, they will have to submit to the form and will not have that same liberty. So it is that the more they learn in this early work which we call The Practice of Texts—the more they learn about the uses of voice, tone, modulation and rhythm before they come up against the "obstacle" of form—the freer they will feel later in their acting.

This use of non-dramatic texts makes it easier for the student to develop fluency and, if treated rightly, he will never forget this free experience and will be able to go on to establish a familiarity with a great variety of texts.

The Reading of Three Plays

In the second part of the second term the students are brought into contact with three different categories of plays: a classical comedy, a classical tragedy and a realistic play. These plays are read in quick succession, two to two-and-a-half weeks being devoted to each. The purpose is to familiarize the students with the differences between these categories, without yet studying or analysing their details. I shall elaborate on this phase of the work in Chapter Seven.

Poetry

In the third term we come to the speaking aloud of verse. We call this branch of the training "l'Expression Parlée" in French; it is difficult to find an English equivalent. In it we strive to find a way of acting without *doing*. In rehearsals of a play our principal interest is in "doing," but in these specialised exercises on poetic texts we are more concerned at first with obtaining a complete expression of meaning through the use of the voice alone; with finding a way of acting which is based, almost entirely, on the use of the *voice*—on tone, phrasing, pace and rhythm.

From the moment when the student in his reading first encounters formal verse or prose with a poetic quality, every effort should be made to awaken within him a feeling for poetry. This early work on verse prepares the ground for all the student's later investigation of plays in the major styles and is, therefore, one of the most crucial moments in the training. It is here that he discovers whether he is or is not responsive to poetry. Later when he comes in contact with a play of great poetic style, either modern or classical, it is only through his *own* appreciation of the richness, the quality, the grandeur of the poet's vision that the student can come close to an interpretation which will do justice to the poetry of the text.

The student must learn that although meaning is expressed through form, form also leads to meaning; meaning cannot always be apprehended by reason alone. The student should be made aware of the essence of poetry and its different elements. He should come to realise that words can be used for their colour and sound, that words shape a line of verse and its beat; he should recognize the imaginative activity in a metaphor, the dramatic power in a poetic image. In fact, many poems and great classical plays can only be approached and appreciated in this way.

In these sessions all the major forms of poetry are used: odes, sonnets, epics, and narratives, various kind of ballads and lyrics. The differences between these forms should be made entirely clear. Starting with shorter verse forms, the student should become familiar with the meter, rhythm, stress and texture of their language. To begin with we concentrate on verse from non-dramatic sources, although this is almost a contradiction in terms, since the heightened language of poetry is, in a very real sense, always truly dramatic.

Considerable thought should be given to the choice of the material used, which should, gradually, grow more challenging. The texts given to the student should be chosen with his specific needs in mind and with the knowledge of his requirements and his particular difficulties of the moment. He must learn how to memorise a poem; and he should begin to know how to shape a speech, find the mood and feeling under the text. He is not shown how to use gestures, but if he feels like it he is free to use them. He should, however, be discouraged from trying to "act," so that his whole attention can be given to speech as such.

As well as the style of the pieces chosen, the teacher should also discuss the individual poets and the times in which they lived and wrote. The student can then relate to the background of a particular piece and to the differences in style in different periods. He should also be encouraged to do research into other aspects of different periods: he should know about the music of the time, the dances that were danced and the clothes that were worn. For this it is very helpful to use the transformable skirt invented by the designers Motley for the Old Vic Theatre School and now used in many parts of the world in drama schools and drama departments of colleges and universities.

This versatile aid allows for transformations of all kinds and is equally adaptable to women and men. It can become a Greek tunic or a Roman toga. It can be transformed into clothes of the medieval period or of the seventeenth, eighteenth or nineteenth centuries; it can be used to form a bustle, or it can be used as a cloak for a man.

Working with this, the student will discover how clothes can convey to an actor the feeling of a given period, how they influence the way he walks, the way he stands, moves, sits and, of course, how, ultimately, they effect the way he speaks.

As to poetry we must teach the student that it is not to be treated as some sort of cultural gimmick, as some precious, unattainable pinnacle, but as part of life. Poetry must be spoken, not declaimed or chanted. I often say to my students that poetry may be a better way of representing reality than photography.

I would like here, in order to emphasize these points, to quote

THE MOTLEY PRACTICE SKIRT

Cut a semi-circle of cloth, preferably of a material which does not have to be hemmed (if a hem is necessary it should be faced). To form the waist, cut a small semi-circle at the centre of the straight side, slightly larger than the waist measurement.

Face the waist to make a slot for the drawstring or tape. Make a slit on the outside of the skirt and insert the tape through this, leaving a loop sticking out. Sew the ends of the tape firmly at A and B.

Sew a trouser hook at one side of the waist and a bar on the other. Sew patent fasteners along both sides of the skirt at C and D, the female ones on the outside and the male ones on the inside.

To wear one skirt only, fasten it directly round the waist with the hook and eye, snap the patent fasteners, and adjust the tape to correct waist size. To wear several skirts at a time, hook them to one another and, using the tapes, adjust the waist size to fit.

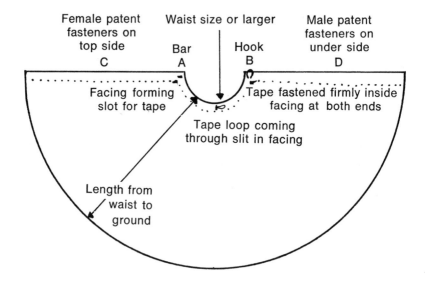

a passage from T. S. Eliot's *Poetry and Drama*. Eliot is a master of realistic poetry; his poetry is an instrument of realism; he uses it to penetrate and to enhance reality:

> What we have to do is to bring poetry into the world in which the audience lives, and to which it returns when it leaves the theatre; not to transport the audience into some imaginary world totally unlike its own, an unreal world in which poetry is tolerated. What I should hope is, that the audience should find, at the moment of awareness that it is hearing poetry, that it is saying to itself "I could talk in poetry too!" Then we should not be transported into an artificial world. On the contrary, our own dreary, sordid, daily world would suddenly become illuminated and trans-figured.

The student should be encouraged to read poetry on his own and particularly to read poetry aloud to others. If the student does this *without* dramatising, if he submits to the character of the poetry, it can bring him to an understanding of the purity of style and its objectivity—provided, of course, he makes an effort to recognise the style of each poem, of each part of it.

It must be understood that poetry must be spoken and speaking poetry in a lively way does *not* mean dramatising it.

At the beginning of the second year we make up a kind of preparatory period in which the student becomes familiar with poetry in all its forms. Later this work moves into the realm of dramatic blank verse, and in the spring term we finally come to the culmination of this part of the training: the reading or speaking aloud of speeches and scenes from dramatic texts, particularly those of Shakespeare.

The emphasis is on the text and on finding the intrinsic reality of a written style. Whereas in rehearsals of a play we are prin-cipally interested in acting and interpretation, in this advanced stage of text-practice we are concerned with speech and its deliv-ery, and a way of acting which we called earlier vocal acting. Through this specialisation, the student will gradually arrive at interpretation, an interpretation stemming from the text.

During this work the student will be shown how to use a text, how, by respecting form, he can achieve meaning and truth. He will also see that form has value in itself. If one attempts to infuse a classical text of great style with a modern reality which is not identical with the formal values of the original, one may end up not only losing the style of the form, but also failing to render the true meaning.

This is particularly significant in our time when, due to various influences, there is a tendency to transform great verse into prose and when—by an over-concern with truth—form, style and poetic value are often destroyed. This is a basic problem which we have to face and one that is extremely difficult to solve.

L'Expression Parlée offers the student a unique opportunity to pause and to work in depth. By concentrating only on the text, without distractions from the technical disciplines, he will have the time to dwell on this significant question of style: the relationship between form and meaning.

This is the only moment in our work on interpretation when we deal with comparatively short segments of texts. In all other areas of interpretation we deliberately avoid working on isolated scenes.

But in the Poetry classes we *do* use scenes and speeches and provide enough time for an examination of the texts to be pushed to a considerable depth. It would be impossible to investigate an entire play so thoroughly during a normal rehearsal period at the school.

The material for this work should again be carefully selected from many different sources and move progressively towards texts of increasing complexity. Use should be made of speeches from the great tragedies and comedies, as well as certain masterpieces of a poetic kind that are situated, as it were, between poetry and theatre. I am thinking here of Milton—*Comus* or *Paradise Lost*, Book I—or descriptive passages from the Bible, or indeed any source that can inspire an actor.

Classes in poetry should be held at least twice a week and they should last about an hour and a half, or, depending on the number of students participating, two hours.

Each student should have at least a quarter of an hour each week when he can be alone with his teacher. At this time he should be given his assignment, and they should together examine the meaning, shape, style and rhythm of the chosen text. The student then works by himself on the piece and delivers it at their next meeting. While this is going on, the other students continue work on their own assignments by themselves until their turn arrives and they deliver their speeches to their teacher for criticism. This work of preparation, help and criticism is repeated as many times as judged necessary by the teacher.

Early on, sessions are spent on blank verse, mainly Shakespeare's; emphasis is placed on the discovery of the mood and feeling under the text as they affect its phrasing and shape. Speeches with a lyrical quality, such as those of Titania and Oberon in *A Midsummer Night's Dream*, of Perdita in *The Winter's Tale*, and of the Goddesses in *The Tempest*, are often helpful. The student's whole attention is given to the delivery of the speech. He must be discouraged from trying to act. Later, as he begins to feel free and confident in his speech, he will begin to act spontaneously.

Comedy and Farce

> Nobody should try to play comedy unless they have a circus going on inside themselves.
>
> LUBITSCH

As a part of l'Expression Parlée, we bring in the study of comedy and farce. This vital moment in the student's training will take place after he has gone through a class called Character Improvisation, a class which begins in the fifth term and which we will describe later.

The work on comedy and farce needs a special vitality and exuberance, a great boldness of invention and considerable physical and vocal technique.

Comedy should be studied because, with its substructure—farce —it stems directly from the very origins of theatre and continues through all the major periods: the Greek, with Aristophanes and the Satyr Plays; the Roman, with Plautus; the Commedia dell'Arte; the Elizabethan, with Shakespeare and his clowns Gobbo, Autolycus, Malvolio; the Spanish Golden Age, with Cervantes and Lope de Vega. And there are the farceurs of the music halls and films, many of whom invented and wrote their own material—Chaplin, Little Titch, Sid Fields, Fernandel, Bert Lahr, Grock—all characters richly and genuinely human.

Comedy and farce with their satirical qualities have always exerted a strong influence on the society they fustigated. During the 17th century came the birth of the Comedy of Manners which gradually acquired a more refined, more subtle style. It continued its development until the end of the 18th century, when it became almost swamped in the bourgeois themes and language of the 19th. Apart from this bourgeois comedy, farce and true comedy continued to chase each other across the realist period; we meet them again and again in our own time.

There is a great variety of language used in comedy and farce which oscillates between prose and verse. With the Greeks the language can be vulgar, satirical, obscene, lyrical or poetic; with the Romans it becomes psychological, it begins to create types; with Shakespeare and the Elizabethans, it becomes enriched with a great variety of poetic images.

As for rhythm, the student of comedy and farce should develop a positive *enjoyment* of it; there are often short, swift passages of repartee, following one another without pause, where the *truth* of character and situation flash like lightning across the stage. There is no time to hesitate; if one does, it kills the acting. There is no opportunity to reflect; this is indeed a school for unerring accuracy. If one slows down, the very meaning of the text disappears. Imagine an *allegro* passage by Mozart played *largo* in slow motion, by a musician who, trying to concentrate on "feeling" every note, thereby destroys the rhythm.

So one sees that the vocal technique needed for comedy and farce is very demanding. The voice must have lightness and swiftness, but also strength and breadth. The actor must have a wide vocal range at his disposal and be able to pass through a whole gamut of tones—for monotone kills comedy.

The actor must also know how to use laughter—a great variety of laughter—and have a technique at hand to produce the kind of laughter needed at a given moment. Here again carefully devised exercises should be given to teach laughter of various kinds.

By this time the student will have acquired a certain vocal facility and agility of tongue, phrasing and articulation, so that more can be expected of him. Now the students work in pairs, since the texts for this phase are chosen to demonstrate the construction and style of speeches and scenes of considerable complexity. They will have to learn how to give shape to a passage by using various rhythms, changes of tone and significant pauses and by using stress on specific words and phrases.

Actually, this becomes an introduction to Restoration Comedy and it is, I think, quite valuable to have such an introduction as early as the sixth term. When the student finally comes to act in a Restoration play—during the ninth term in the third year—the text and the acting will not present him with too many difficulties.

Here again it is useful to go through a series of special exercises to supplement the work in comedy. It is important to find short phrases and sentences from plays which fit the intention of each exercise. Attention must also be paid to lightness of articulation and delivery, and, especially, to flexibility of the tongue.

For this kind of vocal gymnastic it would be helpful for the student to work with his singing teacher on recitatives from Italian operas and similar passages from the work of Kurt Weill or Gian-Carlo Menotti, for example. Music-dramas that include some form of "Sprechstimme" could also be used. These relate directly to the demands of highly structured comedy texts.

During the work on the Practice of Texts, there is a course called Character Improvisation with and without masks, which runs parallel to Poetry and during which, among other skills, the student learns all kinds of physical and speech gags, all of which are particularly helpful in preparing him for his first rehearsal project in comedy and farce.

All this has to be worked on with close attention to projection in the delivery of both words and movement.

Tragedy

In the sixth and seventh term Poetry continues, the main emphasis now being on the study of tragedy: here we choose major speeches from the great classical texts of the Greeks, Shakespeare, the Jacobeans, the Spanish tragedians, Milton, and, nearer our times, T. S. Eliot.

There are few modern tragedies of a stature equal to that of those above mentioned. Tragedy seems to have been replaced by what is now called "drama." Another line in the evolution of tragedy has been towards opera—the link between the two being the voice, the music and the lyrical exaltation.

By now the student will have had an initiation into style and will have become aware of the many varied approaches to different styles; his ear will have become attuned to differences in their musicality, their soul. This is why he must know how to modulate, how to follow the feeling in a given text and be able to play with his voice so that he can express in a direct way the form of the text. He will also begin to recognise whether the quality of a voice is in rapport with the role being acted. The emotional power of a voice must adhere completely to the text and must not be superimposed on it.

In this work the student will feel the need to expand his emotional range and flexibility. He must then be stretched, in order to acquire the necessary ability to sustain the tone of a speech. By now he will also have a more clearly defined sense of style so that we can use this expanded emotional range to communicate and project it more vividly to others.

Students can work alone or in groups of two or three. The organisation of the classes remains essentially the same as in the earlier phases, but supplementary, preparatory exercises are necessary and take on a new importance. Since we are dealing with the intensified emotion of tragedy, usually expressed in a very condensed form of verse, these special exercises are absolutely essential in order to give the student the basic imaginative support necessary to sustain and communicate these emotions. Here we deal with the components of tragedy, the primary themes of courage, honour, revenge, hate, doom and bitter regret. They must be understood and expressed without self-pity in both their choral and individual manifestations.

Supplementary exercises can be used in working on passages from such Greek tragedies as *Oedipus Rex*, *Medea*, *Electra*, *The*

Trojan Women or on soliloquies like that of Thomas à Becket halfway through T. S. Eliot's *Murder in the Cathedral*.

Exercises for tragedy are very difficult and demand an uninhibited attitude; we do not force these strong emotions on the student. If he cannot handle them at the moment, we drop the exercise and return to it at a later time. The reader will have realised by now that I do not believe in forcing anything on a student, but rather I believe in creating a climate in which he can, gradually, arrive at the desired result.

At the beginning of the third year the separate study of poetry—that special study of speech and its delivery—ends and gives way to an intensified study of dramatic texts and to rehearsing plays.

At a later point the student will feel the need for further work in this field and Poetry—l'Expression Parlée—will be taken up again.

Perhaps it would be useful to consider here an example of a French tragedy: *Berenice* by Racine. With its superb text in verse, it was first performed in 1670 in Paris. One of Racine's most motionless plays, it has hardly any visible action. Still, action exists: the play has an emotional *inner* action which has to be conveyed by the way the actor speaks, by the tone of his voice and by an economy of moves and gestures. In such a play as this anything one sees takes on an enormous importance. A still face that suddenly expresses an emotion with a look, two short steps taken toward one another by parting lovers, a hand stretched out to say goodbye—all these make an extremely exciting impact through their economy. The rest lies in the voice, its modulations, its rhythms. This strong inner action, through impulses given by the text at certain key moments, fuses with the physical body.

I mention this here to show what the voice by itself can do to communicate deep feelings without the actor's having to resort to moves or underlining gestures, which can sometimes hinder rather than help. The actor's vocal technique and his use of language should be instruments of knowledge, ways to penetrate to the meaning of a text before any of its words are uttered on the stage.

This is why I strongly urge students not to learn their texts parrot-like, not to be word-perfect when they come to their first rehearsals and not to make their choices about the character merely through thinking about it. Instead, they should let the words of the text come to them gradually, until they are filled with them. The meaning of the words must be given time to penetrate their beings.

As to moves and gestures: mere agitation is not acting. An actor who moves his face all the time does not hold our attention; but when a face has been motionless, and *then* moves, the slightest expression will have great power.

The creative artist cultivates, by appropriate exercises, his imagination and his faculties of observation. He puts his body and mind in a state of total relaxation, nurtures the feelings required for the part by all the contributions that his affinitive memory can make, and learns to conjure up and welcome the physical gestures that will awaken and sustain the inner life of the part.

This chapter contains the fundamental basis for all our future work; it will be useful from time to time during the four years of the training for the teacher to refer back to it.

Walter Kerr in writing about John Gielgud's performance of *The Ages of Man* says:

> . . .Why are we so startled that language divorced from all its customary theatrical companions should move us, and why are we suddenly so willing to submit ourselves to the separated experience? What we seem to be doing is re-examining the basic tools independently of one another, and independently of the 'play' itself. Marcel Marceau plants his feet on the stage and then begins to discover what they can be made to do, as though the very notion of movement needed fresh investigation. . . . Two complementary lines (Gielgud and Marceau) are being extended toward their ultimate boundaries; when their outside dimensions are reached, perhaps they can be fused in the interests of a bigger, and even better play. . . . We are curious about a range to come, and an intensity of vision we may have been missing.

Chapter Five

THE IMAGINATIVE BACKGROUND

How can one look at the past
if not with the eyes of the present?

THE PURPOSE OF THIS part of the training is to give the student/actor
the ways and means of understanding and assimilating the social
and cultural climate of every play, past or present, he will be
asked to interpret. Our aim is to nourish the student's imagination
by giving him a sense of the reality of remote periods and by
helping him see how different theatrical periods relate to one
another historically and aesthetically. Facts should stimulate the
student's imagination to practical action but these facts must always be directly related to the rest of his work at the school.

To introduce students to the imaginative background, we present a series of talks covering salient points in the history of the
theatre, of costumes and manners, of music, dance and the decorative arts, as these relate to the actor. A brief but graphic account
of the evolution of acting spaces, from the earliest times to the
present, is also included. Ideally, these talks should be given by
theatre people; an academic atmosphere should be avoided at all
costs.

Whenever possible these talks should be illustrated with pictorial examples of architecture, furniture and costumes and with
paintings illustrating the manners and the way of life of a given
epoch.

But, more importantly, these short introductions to the culture
of the past and present should provide opportunities for the student to practice ways of behaviour, to manipulate costumes and
personal props, and to learn some elements of the dances and
listen to music of the time.

This work takes place concurrently with the work on the Practice of Texts we just discussed. Continuing practice of this sort helps diminish that uneasiness, that feeling that actors often have when dealing with texts of remote periods that what they are doing is "artificial." Reading and re-reading these texts aloud to others will finally bring the actor to feel at ease with them.

In this way the student is led unobtrusively toward the development of a notion of style by the acquisition of facts and by the application of them in many kinds of practical exercises.

In my earlier book, *Theatre: The Rediscovery of Style,* I suggested that we define style as "the perceptible form that is taken by reality in revealing to us its true and inner character. There is something secret about style. This perceptible or outward form holds a secret which we have got to penetrate if we are to perceive the essential reality which lies beneath it."

It is not easy to acquire style. One cannot acquire it by putting on a costume and hoping that one will be magically endowed with the ability to act a play in a particular style. Without the actor's having practised—physically practised—style, those clothes would look as if they were draped on a coat hanger. The feeling for style must come from an informed imagination. Style is a true product of a way of living and therefore cannot be simulated.

One of our guiding principles is to lead the student toward an imaginative and creative attitude in all aspects of his work, hence the emphasis on imagination in the title of this chapter. But imagination is not enough: there must be a technique for its application, for the *physical* and *vocal* expression of what the imagination knows. It is this physical and vocal knowledge which makes the re-creation of style possible. Imagination without technical skill is a form of impudence.

But to imagination and technique we must add interpretation, for it is one thing to understand the styles of the past and quite another to give them an interpretation which has meaning for today. If we look to the past, it is mainly to find in it not only knowledge but also a source of invention for the present. How can one look at the past if not with the eyes of the present?

Here I am immediately reminded of an incident that occurred in Stockholm during an International Theatre Institute (UNESCO)

Symposium on the Professional Training of the Actor: near the end of a panel discussion a man in the audience of two thousand people suddenly shouted out: "To hell with the word 'style'!" Suria Saint-Denis, who was co-chairman of the conference, answered "To say 'to hell' with this word is the easy way out. One should not be afraid of words. One is faced with students who will ask questions, because they will find these words in books. One cannot just ignore them. One has to accept this and give answers. By simply eliminating such words, one will only put one's students into a difficult and puzzling situation. However, if one says to a student when asked what style is: 'style is life,' then the student will forget about 'style' and will understand that, for instance, at the time of Chekhov, or even Shakespeare, people lived and felt as people do today. We are, after all, human beings: we live, we love, we feel—anything you like—and this was the same for those who lived before us. But we must discover *how* they lived and thought and loved in order to understand them and give life to them before an audience."

I feel it would be appropriate to make it clear once more that I do not mean that only classical plays have style—any valid play has its own style, be it by Sophocles, Chekhov, or Pinter or Beckett. The student/actor of today must study not only the societies of the past but the society he lives in as well.

The first talks should be given in the second part of the first term. The subject of these talks should be the History of the Stage—the development of acting spaces.

The main purpose of this is to draw the student's attention to different kinds of acting spaces and how these differences can affect him in his acting.

In previous chapters I have said that our aim is to form an actor equipped with all possible means of dramatic expression, an actor capable of meeting the demands of today's and tomorrow's ever-changing theatre. And I have also said that whatever experiments may be attempted with new forms of writing, new stages and developing technical devices—everything ultimately depends on the human being, the actor.

It seems therefore important that these talks be concerned

with the significance and the impact of the actor's body in space—the body as the centre of the architectural form it is surrounded by, that is, the stage.

As early as 1957 I said in a BBC talk that the ideal space is one where the stage is thrust toward a compact auditorium—an auditorium in which the different levels of seats are built in a relatively small space so that the row of seats most distant from the stage is still comparatively near its front.

This stage should be made adaptable to various shapes, so that it can serve a great variety of styles, and can bring the scenic action into close contact with the audience, so that the performer's acting—his gestures, his facial expressions and his voice—can be seen and heard by everyone without the actor's having to force.

In this way two worlds—the actor's and the audience's—can, without any hindrance, interpenetrate one another.

This architecture offers all kinds of possibilities for relationships between stage and auditorium; for instance, the actor can advance from that mysterious zone, far back there upstage, and gradually increase in size, as he approaches the audience, until he finds himself in their midst—bringing with him the circumstantial evidence of the drama, which he delivers to the audience with the reserve and economy that proximity permits and imposes (as, incidentally, it did at the time of the Greeks and the Elizabethans).

But this theatrical geography—which has come to us from the magical world of opera—where the quality of fairy-tale enchantment is an important element—and from that world of illusion of naturalistic realism—where we, amazed, are able to participate in other people's secrets in a realm of total intimacy—this geography—is it to be the landscape of the theatre of the future?

This perhaps best describes what I mean by creating a space where the imagination of the poet and the playing of the actor can be in harmony: the one emerging from silence to sound, the other passing from empty space to space coming alive through movement.

How easy it is not to be aware of space until a moving body creates it! An empty space can be a great stimulus to movement and become almost tangible to an actor. For the actor to become able to create his own surroundings and make the un-visible visible is a vital step in the development of his creative imagination.

During the time these talks about the historical development of acting spaces are being given, work related to space should be done in some of the other branches of the training:

- In the movement classes, in order to develop a feeling for precision and direction in space, we sometimes begin with exercises in simple turns—quarter, half and full.
- In Improvisation, when the first simple scenarios are devised, exercises should be done with a precise placing of imaginary furniture within the context of an imaginary room; moves in the room and to and around the furniture should be practiced. Places for entrances and exits should be established in relationship to the setting of that room.
- In the Non-Dramatic Reading sessions, texts which describe specific places should be chosen for the readings.

In this way the student will be made aware of space and develop a feeling for it in all its aspects and thus, literally, widen the horizon of the space immediately surrounding his own body and extend the radius from his center in which he can create and control space.

Let us now consider in more detail what the talks in the first series should cover.

I. *A History of Acting Spaces*

To start with, we might do well to give a short introduction to the earliest forms of "drama" and their acting spaces as, for instance, the Egyptian: their priests believed that the best initiation into religion was through dramas, enacted by priest/actors in open spaces or in temples. After a description of the Egyptian ceremonial festivals, the students would then be led to the theatre of the Greeks and the evolution of Greek drama, which was so intimately related to their acting spaces: Epidaurus, Delphi, the Theatre of Dionysus at Athens, the theatres at Taormina and Syracuse in Sicily among others.

The next talk should be on the stages of the Romans and Etruscans and then on to the Medieval period and the mystery and miracle plays which were performed in the public squares, in front of the great cathedrals and on travelling pageant wagons as well.

Next we come to the early and late Renaissance and, in particular, to the Elizabethan period in England—one of the most glorious epochs in dramatic history. The most famous Elizabethan theatre, the Globe, with its circular shape, did not allow for scenery—it was therefore the perfect space for solo acting.

In Italy the Teatro Olimpico in Vicenza and the Teatro Farnese in Parma are among the finest surviving theatre buildings of the 16th and 17th centuries.

We must not forget the extraordinary influence of the Bibiena family and their perspective designs. During this period there is a tentative approach to the picture-frame stage of the late 18th and 19th centuries.

It should be pointed out that the picture-frame stage greatly changed the way of acting: the orientation of the actor's body, being closed in on three sides, became more frontal.

A brief description of the various developments of the picture-frame stage—that is, the proscenium stage—should be given. This will, of course, include a study of scenery and scenic devices. We should continue to trace this development through the 20th century, when the liberation of acting space from the tyranny of the proscenium arch came about.

Before the end of this series of talks on the history of acting spaces, the student should also be made aware of the theatres of the East: of India, Java, Bali and especially of the acting spaces in the Chinese and Japanese theatres.

We must remember that ours is a teaching for artists. It is not the scholarly aspects which are important, but the ways in which these subjects continually stimulate the student's imagination and relate back to the theatre.

If I have gone into detail on the foregoing subject it is to draw attention to how important the human being—the actor—is in relation to his surroundings; how he is influenced by them, but also how he can influence them in turn.

II. *The History of Drama*

These talks should start in the second term of the first year and cover the drama of:

- The Greek, Roman and Medieval periods.
- Elizabethan and Jacobean England.
- The early and late Renaissance.
- The Commedia dell'Arte.
- The Restoration and 18th century.
- The late 19th and early 20th centuries.
- The Chinese and Japanese theatre.
- The later 20th century.

III. *The Costumes, Customs, Manners and the Arts of the Major Theatrical Periods*

Here the aim is to bring a particular era to life by studying concrete examples, illustrations and audio-visual materials that present the overall life style of that era as revealed in its paintings, sculpture, architecture, music and clothing styles. Its social and political concepts should also be studied.

We should not forget to introduce in this series the society of today and the recent past. I have often been struck by the fact that students sometimes seem to know more about the late 19th century, for example, than they do about the life of twenty years ago.

All this can be accomplished in a meaningful way only by the personal magnetism of a lecturer with the ability to evoke the true vitality of an era for the student/actors.

It seems important to mention here that this work need not be done chronologically, but in relation to the sequence of the play-rehearsal projects.

IV. *Pictorial Documentation*

This phase of the work should start with an informal talk by the director of the play, accompanied by a presentation of pictorial documents related to the specific period of the play about to be rehearsed.

This presentation should consist of photographs of architecture, reproductions of paintings, fashionplates and costume designs, actual costumes and accessories—walking sticks, fans, shoes, handkerchiefs—and props such as goblets and weapons, as well as typical pieces of furniture. It is sometimes useful to include a few items from the immediately preceding period, items that condition and shape the actor's movements, so that the student has an idea of the continuing evolution of fashion and furniture; for instance, the change in the fashion of men's shoes from the early 17th century to the latter part of the same century.

In selecting the materials for such exhibits, one should be guided by the following principle: our object is to present to the student, as accurately as possible, the essential mood and way of life of a given epoch.

From this it follows that we want:

- to show the true style—the crystalization or essence of a given period—in such a way that the objects on display make the period come alive in the student's imagination. As the exhibits could easily become diffuse and thus bewildering, one should avoid showing him too many items.
- to stimulate the student's creative imagination. In order to do this, we insist that objects presented be taken from everyday life and not from the theatre.
- to present an overall view of the way man related to man, as expressed in the life of the time. Inevitably, the physical objects presented to the students will relate to other areas under consideration, such as the political and social climate in which they existed.

Again, everything possible should be done to diminish in the student/actor his feelings of awe and apprehension when considering style.

The teacher should carefully introduce students to the best way of looking at the pictorial material, pointing out what to look for and how to find it. For example, in the case of dress, have the student first look at the general silhouette of the clothes, the way the coiffure was done for women *and* men, the kind of hats they wore, the accessories they carried. Then draw attention to the shape of the furniture, particularly the chairs. Next, relate the clothes of the period to the way people sat on those chairs, how people stood, walked, held their arms and hands. Finally, examine the faces of the people in the illustrations: what can facial characteristics tell us about people of different social strata—the aristocracy, the bourgoisie, footmen, servants, peasants. Discuss in what way these people differ or resemble similar people of today.

It is wise to progress slowly, since too-much-all-at-once tends *not* to be absorbed in the right way. Give the student time to observe precisely. Later in the practical exercise classes, when he himself will actually wear a costume, as he practices sitting down, standing, walking, gesturing and dancing, the image of these documentary materials will gradually come to mind.

Supplementing this, the student should listen to music of the time and visit museums and galleries. He should be encouraged to read books about the period, although, once again, we need not feel we must deluge the student with them. The same guiding principle applies here as in the selection of novels read in the first year: the selection is to be on the basis of their value as imaginative material for an *actor*. This applies also to museum visits: considering carefully one painting of a master artist will give the actor more insight and inspiration than glancing, in quick succession, at many. Such artists as Raphael, Filippo Lippi, Bellini, Pissaro, Uccello or Giorgione are particularly rich sources.

This kind of research will, in time, become almost second nature to the student; it is something whose value he will recognize as it bears fruit in rehearsals.

Some Practical Exercises

To see how the introduction to style might be related to the different play projects, I suggest we deal with one specific style. If it has been determined that in the third year a Restoration comedy will be done in the third term, then for three or four weeks in advance of rehearsals the entire sequence of talks, student research, physical exercises in manners, dances and so forth, will be focussed on the Restoration period. If the first term of the third year is given over to the rehearsal of a realistic, contemporary play and the second to a Greek tragedy, then, in practice, by about the middle of the rehearsal period of the realistic play, preparatory work will have begun on the Greeks, and, in the same way, by the middle of rehearsals of the Greek tragedy, preparatory work and research into practical questions of style will have begun on the Restoration period.

It will be seen that a part of the style practice overlaps the play rehearsals, that is, it runs simultaneously with the first two weeks of rehearsals on a specific play in another style; once the current play is well into rehearsal, an entirely new style practice begins, designed to prepare the student for the subsequent rehearsal project.

Once his imaginative capacity and his expressive means are expanded and strengthened, he will then be able to sustain the range of physical virtuosity and excitement required, for instance, by a Restoration play.

As we have been dealing with the Restoration, I should like to give a few examples of exercises based on that period which were done with students at my schools.

One of the characteristic ways in which people moved in the Restoration period was in *curves*. In order to practice this kind of curved movement, we placed several chairs in a row with just enough space in between them to let the women, wearing their double rehearsal skirts, walk swiftly in and out, in a serpentine pattern, without upsetting the chairs. While doing this exercise the students should feel the swing and the weight of the skirt as they walk. Then the men should do the same, winding in and out between the chairs with swift, elegant moves, their arms—in imaginary elaborate sleeves of the period—slightly raised, with elbows turned out.

Around 1680 the way women held and moved their heads was influenced by the Fontange, a kind of headdress made of several vertical layers of lace worn on top of an elaborate coiffure of large, swirling curls.

The student must understand that we are not trying to *imitate* moves and manners in a purely historical way; we are trying to find the *reasons* why people behaved in a certain way. We concentrate on these reasons and let our bodies naturally find the appropriate balance and posture. Once again, it is a question of imaginative support: if the student understands that it was the custom for men to show off their clothes, that this affected the position of the arms in relation to the waist, the necessity for executing rounded gestures, for tilting the head, will become apparent to him and the movements will come easily and gracefully.

What was taken for granted, what was habitual, in the Restoration, or in any period, has to be made conscious for contemporary actors. They must go through a process of imaginative research to discover the social and cultural reasons for these habits, to determine their meaning and, finally, to experience the pleasure of such physical activity.

As these classes in style progress, students should learn dances of the Restoration: the Gavotte, the Bourée, the Courante and the Minuet. The serpentine exercise is a good preparation for the dance work because through it students will begin to get a sense of the rhythm and tempo of the times as expressed in lightness of motion. In dance classes we also deal with bows, curtsies, and other forms of greeting.

We have been using the Restoration period as an example, but the essentials of physical behaviour are common to all epochs: people sit, stand, walk, run, greet one another; both courtiers and peasants dance and sing.

Incidentally, once the students have started to wear the clothes of a period and have practiced the basic movements, they should no longer be shown pictorial material as this leads them away from re-creation to imitation.

The work on Imaginative Background brings together all the other branches of the training, helps the actor to assimilate them and leads him directly into the play-rehearsal projects, that is, the work on interpretation.

Many of our preparatory exercises make use of the student's growing ability to improvise with and without words. Improvisation plays a crucial role in our work on style. If there is a realistic way of improvising, as the one developed by Stanislavski, then there should be another one for comedy and still a third way for the preparation of the classical plays of great poetic style.

To conclude: we first discover the style of a period through the actual physical life of the time, through the words that were used and then through the emotions involved.

If style is the face of a play, it is also its soul.

Chapter Six

SILENT ACTING—
IMPROVISATION

There are gestures that have a language, hands
that have a mouth, and fingers that have a voice.
A ROMAN POET

IT IS AN ACCEPTED IDEA that speech is the beginning, that it is, in fact, the everything of acting, the only way to convey meaning, emotion and character. This is to ignore completely the richness of the body's physical expression and the fact that this physical expression can often convey much more than speech. Movement—gesture—is an elementary, direct means of expression; our immediate reactions are almost always physical.

The fundamental, the most important branch of our training is Improvisation.

What do we mean by "Improvisation" and why do we attach such a basic importance to it? We believe that through it the student discovers for himself the true essence, the real substance, of acting. It is here that he will find the relationship between the reality of his own inner life, both intellectual and emotional, and its physical expression, the means through which he can convey this reality to others. He must, as it were, first discover *himself*, then bring to the surface what was covered—by education and other factors—and *dare* to show it. This means to give of himself *totally*.

It is during Improvisation that the student should, step by step, become aware of what I like to call his own "inner chemistry," that oscillation between the subjective and objective.

It is here too that he can experience the very fact of acting: this will enable him to connect his work on improvisation with his later work on the interpretation of a text and to use the one for the animation of the other. If as a student he has *fully* experienced this, the imaginative actor will never forget the satisfaction he experienced in finding in himself the essence and the resources of acting. His interpretation will benefit deeply from this creative experience.

He will gradually learn how to arouse his subconscious in such a way that he can safely lose himself in the character he is creating without ever losing the control that concentration and observation have taught him. But this control is only achieved during the latter part of his training, as it demands years of experience.

We do not practice improvisation for its own sake; it is not there to corrupt the text but to invent a way to "uncork" it.

The student will have to learn how to prepare and repeat an improvised scenario just as one repeats a text of a play when performing it, rendering it with complete spontaneity each time.

The student should also come to feel the necessity of bringing to a text the same creative attitude which he has learned from his work in Improvisation.

The contribution which improvisation makes to interpretation is a very vital one: it must be understood that improvisation is a channel through which the imagination flows to reach life in interpretation. The passage from improvisation to interpretation is often a difficult one which takes time to learn to apply.

The work is hard in Improvisation because everything depends on the courage, initiative and invention of the young actor. In contrast to slow, timed research, to overly detailed, intellectual analysis—audacity, inner elation and, sometimes, even excess, can put the student's dramatic imagination into a kind of oscillation which will move him into a zone more propitious to the interpretation of the great styles. The young actor must be helped to discover, on his own, the world of improvisation and be encouraged to love and master it.

The development of the student's faculties of physical expression is of immense importance. To learn how to think, how to speak, with the body and the whole being, how to invent an alphabet of a physical language and how to communicate this language to others, is the truly creative part of the art of the actor.

The Commedia dell'Arte companies consisted of highly trained actors who were able to speak with every part of their body in a great variety of gestures. A famous contemporary Italian company, the Teatro Piccolo of Milan, has developed this tradition to perfection. I remember seeing one of their actors literally talking with his feet in answering a question to which he was not inclined to give a verbal answer! Another actor, in a growing temper of fury and utter confusion, began to stutter and mumble until he finally leapt high into the air in a culmination of helpless rage and exasperation.

But it is not enough to *use* a gesture, this gesture must be inhabited by a thought; gestures not dressed by thoughts are empty and meaningless.

It is only from within one's self, and then only by means of an inspired, *physical* action drawn from one's inner resources, that a character will finally be born.

The work on improvisation is the turning point in the training; it is the most important stage in the development of the creative imagination, the mind and physical aptitudes of the actor.

Some General Considerations

Improvisation liberates the actor's invention and incites him to reach a degree of excellence in his interpretative work which only a creative artist can achieve.

Since the beginning of this century the methods of training actors have undergone constant change until Improvisation now has the central position. Improvisation has been responsible for some of the most dynamic changes in the teaching of movement and voice. Earlier in this century, teaching tended to limit the actor by placing too much emphasis on a habit-forming routine of diction, elocution, declamation, the *literary* study of texts and the "Art of Gesture and Deportment." But by breaking the actor's subservience to the written word, improvisation found a way to liberate these technical disciplines in order to provoke a more inventive "bringing-to-life" of a play.

Today beyond these technical disciplines, which can be enriching if kept flexible, beyond the handling of a text, which is the area of interpretation, the student/actor sees before him a wide and uncultivated field, apparently limitless and, therefore, somewhat threatening. This is the domain of improvisation; its fertility depends completely upon the initiative, selectivity and discipline of each individual actor.

Acting is Action

Through the practice of varied actions, selected from life at the beginning and then transposed more and more into the realm of theatre invention, the student discovers the existence of an inner life whose outer physical expression produces *acting*. By means of practical exercises the student discovers within himself the sources of creative energy which, when properly balanced, will help make his acting authentic, immediate, controlled and free.

Undoubtedly, theatre in its essence is not limited to a written text. It is, therefore, both legitimate and practical not to use texts at first, so that the beginner can better experience his own creative powers. The reader will recall our earlier discussion of the actor/creator and the actor/interpreter: all actors must start with the creative, imaginative attitude of the actor/creator, even though the great majority of them will become actor/interpreters.

We want to bring into being an interpreter who can encompass all aspects of drama, all its different manifestations in every country and every great historical period. I take the liberty of insisting on this point in order to avoid possible misunderstanding and confusion: we aim for a mastery of each and *every* style. The way of working with improvisation towards an interpretation of Chekhov's Madame Ranevskaya is not identical with that which leads to Juliet or Macbeth, to Electra or Oedipus. What we want is a different kind of improvisation for each different style.

Physical aptitudes and aptitudes of the mind and spirit exist, of course, side by side. However, at the start of the training, in order to simplify matters in a realm that can easily become perplexing, it is, I think, sensible to give priority, temporarily, to the development of the physical.

Why develop the physical first? In point of fact, we have no choice. The student has an instrument at his disposal which as yet does not receive and express imaginative impulses adequately. Everything starts from the body or passes through it. It is, therefore, essential that he conscientiously develop his body first. Parallel with the elementary work in movement, the student is going to use his first classes in Improvisation to become aware of his body as a means of expression. Furthermore, he will begin to know his body as the energising force and the regulator of the spirit and the emotions. But he also learns that the body is inert if the imaginative current does not flow through it. He sees that nothing truthful can be expressed or accomplished unless a state of relaxation is created, which is itself dependent upon a state of physical well-being. Eventually a balance and harmony pervades the actor's being—but this is not achieved in a day.

The first stages of the training are devoted to these basic discoveries. The student also attempts to organize the many fragmented impressions he receives, to find out where impulses originate, to sort out from a multitude of images those which are essential to a continuity of action. Having located the center of physical expression, he learns how to make an expressive impulse feed the entire body.

Ways and Means of Working

During the entire first year of training, the principal accent is on silent improvisation: two hours per day are devoted to it, directly following one hour of movement. The student learns to act by improvising; these are his first acting classes.

This early work is done individually in the classroom; in later phases it can be practiced by two or, at most, three people together.

For classes in Improvisation the student is clothed as in movement class: the legs, shoulders, arms and neck as bare as possible. He works not only without scenery but also without furniture or props, though he may use easy-to-move, lightweight stools. He must find a way physically to make others "see" all the non-existent objects on which the action of his improvisation is based, and, at the same time, acquire a precise control of his body's expression in the emptiness of space.

The success of the student's efforts will depend upon his imagination, observation, concentration and on his control of space. The student cannot play tricks with costume or furniture any more than he is allowed, later on, to toy with a text. There is a ruthless bareness everywhere which prevents the student from hiding behind costumes, curtains, or furniture. He must find the physical means of expressing a given action in perfectly clear and explicit terms.

He must have a language of the body and the discovery of this language is intimately related to the development of his physical technique: the ability to relax the whole body or specific parts of it, to maintain balance in awkward positions, to contract the muscles suddenly and at will, to gather energy in the centre of the body from whence it can be released. In short, the student must be in a state of constant physical *availability* from which he can spring into action at any moment.

This training is rigorous and of such importance that, if the student proves unresponsive to this work, he should be asked to withdraw from the school by the end of the first year.

The Student in Action as Himself

It might be useful here to describe the basic elements in the progression of the work on improvisation.

At first the student is asked only to present those elementary activities of everyday life that he is familiar with from his own personal experience. The student is not to invent characters; he is to be himself. He presents the ordinariness of life, but there is sufficient margin here for invention. Because of the absence of real objects, the student is obliged to find the physical means of presenting true reality. But this must be faithfully presented. If the actor is having breakfast, the non-existent table must be at a constant height from the floor in the eyes of the imagination. One must recognize whether the actor is eating eggs or toast and jam, whether what he is drinking is hot or cold. These become exercises in observation, invention and control.

The teacher gives the student his subject matter, but invention of the precise action, the way he is going to show the action in space, the manner in which he gives reality to it—all these problems have got to be solved by the student. The bareness of the rehearsal room makes this work very hard for the student at first; he will need some help and encouragement from his teacher.

The dramatic imagination of the student, so far, is in a comparatively rudimentary state, but it will come more into play and modify the physical representation of the action when specific exterior circumstances, and later, various moods, are suggested to the student. This new phase will make the student feel the interdependence of an idea and its physical expression, without any reference yet being made to the psychology of character.

For many students this stage creates difficulties of enormous proportions; it places them face to face with seemingly contradictory demands upon their feelings and the expression of them. Precision of physical action is continuously called for, even when the rhythm of the action is complicated by new moods or changes in emotions coming to the surface.

To help maintain this precision, certain complementary exercises should be introduced. These involve a return to the observation of the real world, the use of memories and work on rhythm and stage-space. All this is done in order to nourish the physical action and to avoid recourse to cliché, artificiality, or to the use of excessive concentration, which can paralyse expression.

Occupations

The purpose here is to observe different physical types and to present the characteristic actions of a given craft or trade.

Up to now the student has done all his exercises not trying to present a character other than himself; his observations have been of himself in the daily ordinariness of life. In this new phase, he is asked to observe and show characteristic professional movements of various tradespeople: hairdressers, tailors or dressmakers, mechanics, waiters or waitresses. It is still not a question of specific human beings and yet, by working on an "occupation," a physical change does take place in the student which significantly reshapes him. It is important that the gestures and attitudes of the trade be specifically observed and grasped, that they be presented in the improvisation without the help of real objects, and that they belong only to a man or woman of one particular occupation and could not belong to any other. This is an exercise in capturing the essence of the way a professional moves in his job; a way of moving which may amount to virtuosity. But what is presented must be absolutely real, to both actor and audience.

Once the student has worked out and is able to present the characteristic movements of the craft, he should be asked to do the same again while adding certain clearly defined elements:

- The *place* where he is.
- Once he has established that, he should add a specific *mood* he finds himself in and see how this affects his rhythm.
- Then he should do the same exercise in the same place and in the same mood but add an *incident* which should change his mood and, consequently, his rhythm. He could try different moods and see how they affect his actions and rhythms in different ways.

The teacher should stop the exercise if it seems to be leading the student into a kind of self-imposed theatricality lacking in truth.

These exercises must stay in the realm of great simplicity and be very short—never more than six to ten minutes.

The Scenario

The purpose here is to learn to build up a scenario and repeat it again and again while keeping it spontaneous and alive.

Now we move on to more complex improvisations. Although the subject matter is given by the teacher it is left to the student's own invention to discover how best to compose a scenario. He learns how to place the action on the stage and how to plan the length of each part; how to keep the improvised scenario alive, how to sustain it and make it spontaneous each time it is repeated.

A mistake that is often made about improvisation is to think that people improvise everything in front of an audience. This is simply not true. They do not. The best comedians, like Sid Fields, rehearse their improvisations as long as actors rehearse a play, or a scene from a play—until the time comes when the thing is set. By "setting" everything, they have the freedom to improvise in detail within the framework of their scenario. They then are free to renew their feeling and keep the acting constantly spontaneous.

The teacher and the student should start by examining the chosen subject to be sure that the material is conducive to such a scenario exercise. A complete *visible reality* must be convincingly expressed in the rhythm of life on the stage.

The student will soon discover the pleasure of being able to make visible an invisible world by means of movement.

The purpose of this improvisation is to learn to observe reality, not superficially, but in depth, in order to give the student the habit, right from the start, of evoking reality through his memory of it. This observation in depth will help his invention and be readily available when later he calls upon it in his work.

There should be a certain amount of preparatory work before beginning to "rehearse" the scenario. The student should ask himself:

- How should the scenario be placed?
- What are the precise circumstances?
- Where do they occur?
- What is the mood?
- How does the action develop?

The student should then work separately on each distinct part of his scenario. The teacher should help only in response to specific difficulties of the student. He should do it without explaining too much, without dwelling on theories which may weigh on the student's mind. In short, he should take care not to disturb the student's immediate experience and enjoyment of the work.

Contrary to what was said about the experienced comedian, the student, without setting it too much, and while keeping it flexible, should be sure of each part of his scenario before he starts to put it together.

Once the scenario has been well rehearsed and shown to either the teacher or to some of the other students, he should run through the scenario again, cut some things, and improve on others; in general, he should make sure that the various parts work. He will begin to understand what rehearsing means; he will learn how to repeat something over and over again, always trying to find ways of renewing himself and recapturing his first joys of discovery.

Doing this he will come up against some of the chief problems of acting; in attempting to resolve them, he will also learn something about the construction of a play, and of the scenes within a play.

The Teacher's Approach

> Imaginative teaching is not telling somebody what to do, but guiding him to *experience* it. This continues through the different phases of the evolution of the training and opens for the student ever-widening vistas.

This is a good moment to pause and consider the teacher's approach to the training. He must be prepared to help the student at any moment, but not too readily. During this first phase of the work on silent improvisation the student works for himself; he is in no way concerned with performing. Students should be encouraged to watch and criticize each other's work, but in a constructive and helpful way. Often beginning students watching silent improvisations are carried away by their own imagination and criticise what they *imagine* they see, rather than what they *really* are seeing.

Since other teachers will visit these classes from time to time, it is natural for the student to imagine himself under constant scrutiny. But the student must be reminded that, at the moment, he is working only for himself. In time he will see that the difficulties he is experiencing, while very much his own, are, in fact, the basic difficulties of acting.

As the progression develops, these difficulties increase. As he adds variations of circumstances and moods to his scenarios, the student will discover that mere imitation is inadequate. He will begin to feel a need to concentrate within himself and he will find that his work has to be based on his *own* experience of life; that is to say, it is based on memory fed by *all* his senses. He should also develop the habit of constantly observing others. It is here that the codification of Stanislavski can be very useful, on condition that the jargon-vocabulary that has grown up around his work be avoided and the elements from his system be selected in accord with the particular needs of each individual.

The teacher must be kind, but ruthless, demanding from everyone accurate observation and complete sincerity in his work. Clichés and short cuts towards theatrical effects must be eradicated. But originality, without extravagance, should be cultivated.

Transformation

> The actor has only himself as an instrument. Starting from himself, he must learn how to modify this self and make the transformation visible.

One of the greatest actors of our time, Laurence Olivier, has the astonishing facility, *and* skill, of transforming himself from role to role. He can appear tall or small, fat or thin, he can become an old man or a young one. His body shrinks or stretches according to the role he has to act. All this he accomplishes by sheer physical control.

And then there is Alec Guinness, who has great powers of transformation, particularly evident in his many films. He is often absolutely unrecognisable.

It was said of Eleanora Duse that she had this incredible faculty of transforming herself while acting. She *was* whatever the part she acted demanded of her. She was beautiful, but she could be ugly; she could be tall, she could be small; young or old, light or heavy. She had such a command over her muscles and nerves—her whole body—that it obeyed her slightest intention. One never noticed technique. She would walk from one side of the stage to the other, floating, and one would wonder how she got there.

For most actors their own nature comes first, but with Duse it was different—her "nature" disappeared and she became completely the dramatist's creature.

I write of these three remarkable beings in order to indicate why we attach such importance to this new phase of our training.

The actor who can modify his physical self will be able to approach a role through *physical* images, and then, enriched by this, be able to enter fully into the text. The ability to transform oneself leads to the creation of a character with distinctive traits, rather than just the presentation of a person—an actor—in a specific role.

To begin with, the student is asked to find ways of transforming himself into a person whose nature, temperament and physique are as far removed from his own as possible, and of giving a convincing impression of this specific physical type. The choice of the subject for this transformation depends on the nature and temperament of each student. For example, if he is short, he should attempt to make himself tall; if thin, he should become fat; if delicate, full-blooded; if nervous, lethargic. He need not sustain the transformation for longer than five minutes but he must do it without the aid of costume, padding, props or make-up. The student must not try to think the transformation through intellectually; he must just *make it visible*.

He then chooses various moods and exterior circumstances which would be meaningful for the chosen physical type and works on the transformation under those conditions: a fat person on a hot day, a fat person bending down to lace his shoes, a fat person getting on a bus.

The student can experiment with two opposed ways of accomplishing the transformation: sometimes starting from the physical, he works from the appearance and behaviour which he imagines to belong to his selected type and develops his actions from there; sometimes starting from an inner feeling, he concentrates on the characteristics of this new personality that he is creating in himself until he can translate them into their outer expression. He will decide which way of working appears most fruitful for him; but he should not draw hard and fast conclusions from this. He must never reduce *anything* to routine.

Later on the student will be asked to work with specific characters from plays written in different styles, styles that demand a versatility from the student in dealing with a wide variety of transformations.

There are many exercises which can help the student achieve a physical transformation of his shape while also creating a mood that will colour his behaviour:

- Starting from himself, the student does an exercise such as putting on his socks and shoes in the morning.
- Then, how would the character he has to play, for instance, Sir Peter Teazle in *The School for Scandal*, put *his* shoes on if played as a fat character? His shoes would have high red heels and buckles; how would he handle them? How would he manage his coat with its elaborate shape and its embroidered sleeves with lace cuffs?
- Or how would Chekhov's Uncle Vanya put on *his* shoes or *his* coat? In what ways would he do it in different moods?
- Here again the student has to start from himself and his own habits. But gradually, the man who puts on tight jeans, a polo neck sweater and heavy snow-boots every morning will be able to adapt his everyday movements to what is necessary to dress accurately and convincingly the character he will have to act in a play.

These may seem simple exercises but they are difficult to do. The object is to achieve a wide variety of transformations.

Of course, there are many other facets of transformation. One's body can shrink or one can grow into a huge monster of some kind. One can use only a part of one's body, like a leg or an arm or a hand and fingers, and transform it into whatever one's imagination dictates. A scenario might be invented in which the student starts as an inanimate object, then becomes a similar-in-shape human being and, finally, transforms himself back into the inanimate object.

One of my students once worked out a scenario in which he transformed an imaginary object into a series of different things. At first he amused himself with an imaginary rope in a kind of game. Then the rope seemed to become a snake which tried to encircle him. Then it again became the rope. The fright he had had on encountering the snake caused him to climb up the rope in order to escape from the snake—only to find that the upper end of the rope had turned again into the snake's head; whereupon, he slithered down the rope and began again to play games with it.

There are infinite possibilities for invention. For the student to achieve the imaginative physical skills by which transformations can be accomplished is an important objective of the training. Such skills are very enriching and much needed by the profession.

Animals

> D. W. Griffith advised me to watch animals as much as people, to try to find out how they communicate with each other—*without words.*
>
> Lillian Gish

This series of exercises allows for the most complete and striking transformations, which go much further in the physical modification of the self, and oblige the student to explore unknown regions of his imagination. These exercises transform the student into something very far from himself and this sometimes can have a profound influence on his later work.

For the exercise to be successful and useful, the choice of the animal is crucial. According to his nature and temperament, the student, with the help of his teacher, selects an animal with which he feels a certain affinity; certainly not one which might disturb him too much emotionally.

To start this work of transforming his body, the student begins by precise observation of the chosen animal or by activating his memory of animals he has seen. He must not reduce these observations to the obvious, but rather *select* those elements that can register on the stage and which capture the temperament, the essence of the animal. He must not try *to be* the animal in the abstract; he must get the feeling of the animal in his body and *lend himself* to it.

He should choose a certain action and mood natural to the animal. The action should be simple; just to cross from one end of the room to the other should be sufficient.

He must work in detail to establish his transformation *physically:* how does this animal stand? or run? what kind of mood can be given to it? where does it live? The student must decide on an action and sketch the moves lightly. If he does a four-legged animal, for instance a horse, he must synchronise the movements of the four legs as he walks or trots; he should explore the way a horse holds and moves its head; how, really, does a horse snort?

It is not necessary to do such animals on all fours; sometimes they are best represented by working on two legs, as I once saw a student do a cow. Standing on her two legs, with her torso slightly bent forward and with her arms hanging down, the student established the cow by making a kind of comment on the cow's body: the way she chased insects away by a movement of her head; the way she munched her food, with an inward look in her eyes. The cow was completely believable.

Animal exercises allow the most complete, striking transformations because the subjects are tangible and very distinct from human nature. All will go well if the choice of the animal is right and if the student's concentration, though intense and focused, remains light.

We are, as a matter of fact, stretching Stanislavski's concept of concentration to its limit. Realism is a logical result of such concentration. But, in this exercise, we have moved far beyond realism.

The Entertainers

> He who is interested in neither the theatre nor the
> circus is not a Christian or a pagan—but a fool.
> GEORGE BERNARD SHAW

In this new phase the student will use performers—the world of entertainers—to investigate another kind of transformation that can help him to develop into a versatile performer. These are, perhaps, not in the strictest sense transformations, but they are certainly related.

In the theatre an actor portrays a character. The actor must make him plausible to us; we have to believe in and identify with the character. The actor does not exhibit himself in the same sense that, for instance, the circus performer, the magician or the music-hall entertainer does. These exercises give the student/actor the opportunity to study people who perform in another kind of theatrical dimension.

The work on this subject comes at the moment when the student's imagination has begun to liberate itself, and when he has begun to learn something about projection. The student must start from his inner existence as strongly as ever, but he is drawn out of that by the demands of the entertainer's specialised actions, actions which transcend the boundaries of ordinary life and call for a kind of virtuosity.

Observation, concentration, imagination, physical skill and rhythm are all put to work here, in a world of a quite different specific gravity from the real world. The student now prepares to create a world of fiction. To "live his part" is no longer his problem; he departs from reality and creates his own world, one that is made up more of physical expression and invention than of psychology. In doing this he exercises his faculty to believe in make-believe and develop the ability to *make* his belief believable.

The student's work is becoming more complex. It is possible for him to "live" his presentation of an ordinary occupation, but in the realm of the entertainers this is not possible. Here the student's object is to give the impression of reality to his presentations of performers whose art requires great technical virtuosity, a virtuosity the student probably does not possess, but, with the help of illusion, he may convincingly suggest. Accuracy of observation, concentration and sincerity are no longer enough. An element of fantasy, almost magic, now invades reality and this should give the student a sense of exhilaration. He is asked to represent as many different kinds of entertainers as possible. Sometimes, excited by this world of illusion, he might push a transformation beyond its believable limits. But it is often more valuable in a learning situation to go beyond the limits than to lack the courage to do so.

The progression of the work should be as follows:

- The particular sort of entertainer is chosen and his characteristics and his "tools," if any, established.

- Then the place has to be decided: is it in a circus, a music-hall, an outdoor fair?
- The entertainer's particular mood is chosen.
- The plan of action, the scenario, is devised.
- The complete scenario is rehearsed.

To establish the entertainer's character should be the first object of the work, as everything else is conditioned by this. The student then works objectively, cooly, on all the rest of the different parts of his scenario in separate sessions without setting the parts too soon; for if he gets too committed to his plan, he may limit the flow of his invention. It is only when all the details of character, place, mood and action have been established that the student should put his scenario together and rehearse it.

Here is a scenario done by one of my students:

- A tightrope walker, in mid-course of his act, has a day-dream and thinks himself a bird. Using his imaginary balancing pole to suggest the wings of the bird, he takes off from his tightrope.
- He goes through the particular actions of flying, finding a way to do them with light, gliding steps. Flying around, turning in the air, enjoying his freedom, he suddenly finds himself back on the tightrope doing his routine performance as a tightrope walker.

This was like a split-second day-dream and completely convincing. The observer should actually feel the exhilaration of freedom this flying would give an entertainer released from the routine of the circus act he has to perform daily.

In such a scenario the student has to find a transition between his real world and his dream world, a way to leave and come back to the tightrope act. Perhaps he awakes from his day-dream, nearly losing his footing on the rope. Or the transition could be accomplished by the bird landing on the ground. It feels something sharp under its feet, like the edge of a rock. The bird nearly loses its balance; it instinctively raises its wings and, as the performer awakes from his dream, the bird's wings become once again his arms, holding the balancing pole; he is back in reality, trying to balance on the rope. It is important to find a plausible way of making this transition in a split-second and it must be immediately clear to the observer.

Day-dreams lend themselves easily to similar scenarios and have many possibilities.

The Dream

> The purpose is to go from the reality of life to a dream-reality thereby extending the limits of imagination.

We now take the transformation exercises even further away from everyday reality into the world of dreams. Here one can make use of all possible transformations:

- walking on or through water
- turning into fire
- walking on air or through clouds
- becoming a star in the firmament
- committing a murder
- becoming Alice in Wonderland
- using Lady Macbeth's sleep-walking scene
- taking Macbeth's banquet scene as a point of departure

In doing the dream exercises the student must establish the difference between the life of real action and the life of dream action, each of which has its own logic. One might describe this as a kind of gymnastics, involving two kinds of realities. It is up to the student to indicate the moment of transition when the dream begins and ends; this might be done by a change in the rhythm of the action or the way the body moves.

The scenario for this sort of exercise should not last more than eight to ten minutes, as one must avoid the risk of excessive concentration: the dream could become a nightmare if based on too personal a subject and pursued too far or too long. There is a moment when the flow of the actor's own inner life is freed by the objective demands of the work at hand, but if he allows himself too deep an involvement it may lead him to a kind of excess which he and his teacher might find difficult to control.

These dream exercises are most enriching for an actor and time should be allowed for exploring their possibilities.

We are now at a point in the progression of the teaching where the subjects of the exercises require a considerable breadth of imagination, invention and physical prowess. They prepare the actor/student for those styles which are not naturalistic. However, we must prevent the idea from arising that there is only one way of proceeding. Should that happen, we run the risk of missing our goal, which is to train the student to become as creative as possible in the interpretation of all styles.

In this phase in our work we touch upon a way which leads to an unlimited freedom of the imagination and a poetic spontaneity of acting.

Group Improvisation

> The purpose is to help the students become sensitive to the presence of one another and conscious of their respective positions in space, to make them aware that they are acting together.

Group Improvisation starts in the third term, at the same time the work with the so-called Basic Masks begins.

After all the concentration on individual work in the preceding two terms, now individual feeling and action gives way to group feeling and action. As relationships develop between individuals within the group and as their antennae become more sensitive, the students begin to learn how to act *together*, at first in exercises involving small groups of two or three, then in larger ones.

In the early phases of the work, the student explores two main aspects of his existence within a group. *First:* how to resist the herd instinct. In attempting this, he becomes aware that even inside a crowd there exist separate relationships by which each person maintains his own individuality. *Second:* how to control his own expressive impulses so as to sustain the impact of the group by feeling and reacting *as one* with the others.

The actor must simultaneously preserve his individuality and maintain his responsibility to the group as a whole. He contributes individually to the ensemble without imposing himself. In this way is achieved the creation of a *group* expression, whereas earlier, in the work in Silent Improvisation, the emphasis was almost entirely on the creation of individual expression.

Although the major part of this work will revolve around the development of scenarios, rich and complex in subject matter, certain preliminary exercises must be done before the students can embark upon group improvisations *per se*. These preparatory exercises are in the use of space, memory of space, and the spontaneous transmission of feeling through a group. By these exercises the student acquires something rather close to a sixth sense, something quite different from intellectual remembering. When they become able to sense what is going on around them without actually having to look, the students will easily know their own position on the stage and how that position relates to the other actors. Then unnecessary small moves, almost always prompted by an insufficiently developed sense of space and distracting from the central action, cease and cohesive group movement is achieved. In time, all changes of position on stage will be done by students without any direction from outside, the impetus coming from the sensitivity established within the group.

Here are some preparatory group exercises:

A group of five or six students stand *close* together, their feet firmly planted on the ground, their bodies relaxed and just touching and their eyes *closed*. As they become aware of one another, they slowly begin to sway from one side to the other, then backwards and forwards, never so much that they cannot keep their balance. Soon there will develop a sense of having become "one" and, with this awareness, the swaying will become concerted and smooth. They let the moment happen without analyzing it.

This exercise needs great concentration: it is slow and has to be done for some time before the fusion of individuals into a whole takes place.

A variation of this exercise is to add soft humming to the swaying—it should sound like a gentle wind rustling through bushes and trees.

This exercise can then be developed into the following: the group sways gently, while humming softly; gradually the group increases the volume of the humming while continuing to sway. The crescendo of humming continues, the swaying increases until the group, rushing forward, fans out and comes to a stop with a shout.

All these changes in action must be done without any command from outside; the impetus for the changes and crescendoes will come from within once the feeling of oneness has been established.

A more difficult variation of this exercise occurs when the group begins to move slowly in one or another direction—still with their eyes closed—somehow sensing a "leader" and following him.

Another preparatory exercise could be something like this: a group of people stand in a shallow, flat-bottomed ferry boat and are taken across a river by the ferryman. The group will, together, have to establish that they are all standing on the same moving object which gently moves up and down, as they are being rowed forward. The ferryman propels the boat by thrusting his long pole against the bottom of the river. The jerking of the boat's movement will give the group the rhythm of their concerted action.

An elaboration of the above exercise could be: a small river steamer passes the boat and the waves rippling over the water make the ferry boat rock—nothing violent, but enough to disturb the people's balance. It is important that they all react to the same waves.

After that, a larger steamboat, producing stronger waves, could be used. This boat, passing fairly near, frightens one of the passengers who, losing his balance, upsets the balance of the others. The boat begins to rock dangerously. Finally some of the passengers fall into the water. There are those who laugh and think this funny while others are frightened.

Then, some other group exercises, these having to do with eyes—eyes that see the same thing at the same time:

- In the country, following a train moving against a far horizon.
- At an airfield, watching an airplane doing stunts.
- At a racetrack, watching the running horses passing again and again.
- At a tennis court, keeping eyes on the moving ball.

The main purpose of all these exercises is to work on *concerted* action.

Actually, the student will already have had some experience of this kind in his movement classes during the first and second terms. In those classes almost everything is done as a group and that promotes a common feeling. But those exercises, organized primarily to develop a *physical* sense of rapport between the body and space, are mostly of an abstract kind in so far as they are only occasionally based on a dramatic idea. They do not demand the degree of concerted action that these present exercises do.

Practically speaking, the work in Group Improvisation becomes a school for ensemble playing, but this is not limited to acting or speaking in unison. It has direct application to the great tragedies, such as those of the Greek and Far Eastern theatre, where choral odes and episodes have long been an established tradition. As in Eliot's *Murder in the Cathedral*, the modern theatre has re-introduced individual or group choruses as a viable, dramatic element of the stage action. Therefore, students must be prepared to work as a chorus which has to move together, to speak, sing and even dance together.

The work now enlarges and scenarios should be devised of a wider scope; such subjects as "The Crossing of the Red Sea," a mining disaster, a shipwreck, a labour strike or a lockout might be used. The initial idea can come from the students, but the plan of the scenario should be devised by the teacher with the students to insure that the *group* remains the protagonist of the action and not any individual within the group.

If words are used, they should be selected from an existing text, in order to guarantee a certain quality. Yet, it must be remembered that the scenario should be predominantly mimic in nature. It can be accompanied by music and can use the improvised language we have described earlier. But this *grummelotage* must function dramatically within the scenario; it should be able to give precise and clear meaning to any particular moment of the action. *Grummelotage* springs from the action and blends with it, reinforcing the scenario and giving it also an audible expression. It is the music of meaning.

Subjects can come from many sources; there are no limits to which these kinds of scenarios cannot be taken. I have often thought that we should pursue this work at a higher level in an Advanced Studio devoted to specialised forms of improvisation. Selected actors, who have finished the basic four-year training programme, joined by especially gifted members of the profession (including dramatists, directors and designers) would become the nucleus of such an experimental ensemble. Group Improvisation, more than any form, opens the way for experiments in new genres which can deal with subjects of unlimited dimensions. In fact, Group Improvisation contains all the other forms of theatrical invention: silent improvisation, mime, comic routines, dance, song, group speech, *bruitage musical,* and, of course, improvised dialogue.

This kind of collaboration would take place at the very source of invention, that is to say, in a practical working situation on the stage itself. Such a Studio would be the best school for playwrights in their search for a style; this is so by virtue of the unique way in which scenarios for Group Improvisation are devised. It is the way André Obey and I collaborated on *Noah* with the Compagnie des Quinze.

Ideally such scenarios should be planned by director and dramatist. At first, the scenario is just a loose proposition, offering the actors the maximum range for their invention. The scenario is broken into short scenes and members of the ensemble are assigned to work on them in small groups. The actors establish the existence of their characters and the general mood; then they devise physical actions and the sound patterns of the scenes, perhaps using selection from an existing text, adding, if they like, *grummelotage.* The actors are in complete charge of this phase; once they have seen the result of the actor's work the director and dramatist will tighten the individual sequences and give shape to the entire scenario. The play is born *on the stage* under the guidance and control of both the director and the dramatist.

The designer will serve the dramatic action by providing at

first only the essential elements that intimately relate to what the actor is *doing*. Working in close contact with the improvising actors, director and dramatist, he will later be able to change, adapt or re-invent these elements.

A musician, by his sounds and music, collaborating from the beginning of the improvisational work, can often enhance the actor's speech and shape his rhythms, and through this clarify and *reveal* the meaning of what the actor is trying to invent.

If scenery and costumes and music can spring from such improvisations, so can a text. The experience of this improvisational growth of a play, instigated by the actors, is of great value to a dramatist. He can see how a text can come from their invention, invention that is deeply rooted in the actor's senses and his inner state. If the dramatist absorbs this improvisational experience rightly, he will not write words which come exclusively from the mind; he will be able to write words that will also be the results of living and therefore be much more actable.

These then could be the elements of a contemporary theatre.

It has always been interesting to see how other artists have been attracted to the potentials of this mode of composition: Peter Brook did *US*, a show on the Vietnam War, for the Royal Shakespeare Company in London; Joe Chaikin's Open Theatre in New York used it in *The Serpent*. Richard Schechner's work in this area culminated in his *Dionysus 69* at the Performing Garage in New York; and, of course, there are the experiments of Grotowski based upon classical and contemporary mythology and history, which I saw first in Warsaw in 1963.

The importance of this specialised work cannot be overestimated.

The Mask

The mask enables the actor to experience in its most startling form, the chemistry of acting.

The use of masks in the training of actors had its origins in an incident that happened many years ago at a rehearsal at the Vieux Colombier Theatre, when a young actress held up a rehearsal because she could not overcome her self-consciousness and express her character's feelings through the appropriate physical actions. Tired of having to wait for her to relax, Jacques Copeau, the director, threw a handkerchief over her face and made her repeat the scene. She at once relaxed and her body was able to express what she had been asked to do. This inspired incident led to our exploring the possibilities of mask work in the training of actors. We found that by covering his face with a mask, the actor was often able to forget his inhibitions and to go beyond his usual limits. While it increased the power of his physical expression, it at the same time taught him economy of gesture. It encouraged him to dare to communicate without the help of words. This was, indeed, a valuable discovery.

To us, a mask is a temporary instrument which we offer to the curiosity of the student in the hope that, through literally *shielding* his timidity, it may help his concentration, diminish his self-consciousness, strengthen his inner feelings and lead him to develop his physical powers of outward dramatic expression.

Mask work is central to the training precisely because it enables the student to warm his feelings and cool his head; at the same time it permits him to experience, in its most startling form, the chemistry of acting. At the very moment when the actor's feelings beneath the mask are at their height, the urgent necessity to control his physical actions compels him to detachment and lucidity.

We do not wish in any way to imitate the Greeks, the Japanese or the Chinese, nor use masks that seem copies from a past tradition. The basic masks should be specifically designed for this work and be of normal human size with distinct features, representing the four ages of man:

- Adolescence
- Adulthood
- Mature Age
- Old Age

They must not be abstract, but they must be clear and easy to read from a distance.

It is the concrete experience of the mask which counts more

than anything else. The student must go through this experience in good faith, leaving himself open to all its possibilities. What we are trying to do is to make the student discover inside himself the forces which will allow him to bring to light *reality* in all its fullness; that is to say, the luminous reality of the stage. In order to do this, words are not sufficient.

A mask is a tangible object. It is a presence which encounters one's own—face to face. By the imposition of such an external object on one's face, one will actually feel possessed by a foreign presence, without, however, being dispossessed of one's own self. When one puts a mask on one's face, one receives a strong impulse from it which one must learn how to obey naturally. Because one's own face is not seen, all expression depends on the body, but this expression cannot be released in a valid and dramatic way except by complete concentration on, and openness to, the sensations created by the mask. In other words, in these exercises the mask is the energising force.

Once the actor has acquired the elementary technique that is needed in using a mask, he will begin to realize that masks dislike agitation, that they can only be animated by controlled, strong, and utterly simple actions which depend upon the richness of the inner life within the calm and balanced body of the performer.

The student must not try to force himself to do anything interesting or fantastic; what he does must be simple and clear. The mask obliges him to eliminate everything unnecessary.

As his inner feelings accumulate behind the mask, the actor's face relaxes. This, together with his awareness that his eyes and facial characteristics are concealed as well, will help to simplify his physical, outward expression at the same time that it is being utilized to the utmost.

Without question this work is an excellent introduction to playing classical drama: it is a preparatory school for the tragedy and drama of the great styles.

A mask is an inanimate object that can have no life without the actor's existence; the mask absorbs the actor's personality, on which it feeds. Behind the mask the actor's inner feelings group themselves as in a closed container. Submission to the lesson of the mask helps an actor of talent to master a broad, inspired and objective way of acting. This has, in fact, been the aim of all our previous exercises in improvisation, but probably it has never been realised before with this much clarity and power.

The first encounter with a mask is crucial and, if wrongly handled, can confuse the student. First, have him look for a while at the mask in his hand, then let him put it on. The moment he feels the mask on his face, something should happen to him. He should not look at himself in the mirror with the mask on; he looks at the mask only when it is in his hand. He should keep the *memory* of the mask in his mind, *not* the reflection in the mirror, because, if he relies on the mirror-image, he will act what he *sees* and not what he *feels*.

During the initial phase of the work, he will become aware of the effect of the mask on others. He will also begin to understand the necessity of "lending" himself to the mask.

In class the students should try on the various masks in quick succession, experiencing the effect that different masks can have on them. Then they can decide upon the one they would like to work with. The selection of the right mask is obviously important; students may have to be guided in their initial choice. It is very important for the actor to select a mask that can inspire him; not all masks will have the same effect on each person. And it is also important that the mask fit the face. It may have to be adjusted by using different lengths of elastic headbands and placing foam rubber cushions inside the mask in order to support it properly and reduce any pressure on the face.

Once the working mask has been chosen, some of the elementary principles of mask work should be introduced to the students:

- The smallest movement of the head, the slightest turn, a look up or down, counts.
- Sudden movements, or violent ones, prevent the audience from reading the moment clearly.
- It is important to be aware of the most favourable angle of the mask in relation to the position of the body. If one turns the head too far, the illusion of the mask being part of the body is destroyed—one sees the edge of the mask.

- The same applies, of course, to throwing the head back exposing one's own chin under the mask.
- The sound of breathing under a mask is greatly amplified: one should not hear it. If the student is relaxed his breathing will be quieter.
- To achieve its fullest expression, the mask needs action. But until he gets the feeling that he has become one with the mask, the student should try out simple actions only: walking back and forth, sitting down, watching something or somebody, picking up an object.
- There are certain gestures one cannot do in a naturalistic way with a mask—picking one's nose, for example. But one can find a way to pick one's nose which will involve a certain transposition from everyday life.
- In general, one must find the right sort of technique to make the mask express what it wants; this bears analogy to the technique one uses with a text where one gets the meaning from the text and not from one's own subjectivity.

Let me briefly describe a short demonstration I gave to a group of young actors to introduce them to mask work. Putting on the adult mask, I just walked around aimlessly; I stopped, looked at the group of actors watching me, and walked on. Suddenly, I saw some imaginary thing on the ground, I focussed on it, then lost interest and walked off. Next, I tried the adolescent mask. I followed approximately the same scenario as before, but my expression had become more insolent; my moves had more purpose; I seemed to be more sure of myself. Actually I had not planned any of this; I simply worked from a mixture of what the mask gave me and the memory of what it looked like when I held it in my hand. I let the idea come from the mask rather than imposing an idea *on* the mask.

I then put on the mature mask. This led to more authority—a heavier walk, a more thoughtful look. The general quality had changed; it had become even more aggressive, more definite. I then made a decision: I gave an order to some "off-stage" person. I was disobeyed, so I went off after him.

When I put on the old man's mask, my entire tempo changed yet again; the walk was influenced by the mask; the arms and hands hung and moved quite differently.

The student starts to work by himself with his chosen mask;

later on he can try exercises with two or three other students. His first scenario should have a contemporary subject based on his own experience. As in all improvisation exercises, the circumstances must be detailed and specific, but here, the subject matter, its mood, its external conditions, the character's reality, must be drawn *from* the mask and must be capable of being expressed *through* the mask.

The scenario must not be too precise in the beginning; room must be left for the actor's invention. Once the basic outline of the scenario has been established and appears to be right, the student begins to work with the mask on. Then he does it again with the mask off. He may find that his scenario's original outline will have to be altered to accomodate new things which develop during these two contrasting run-throughs.

The student must look at the mask until he feels permeated by its expression. This sometimes takes a long time. Once he has placed the mask on his face, the student should go into action only when he has *really* felt the mask's impact.

As the student gains experience with masks, he will be in a better position to understand some of the lessons to be learned from them:

- The *body* of the actor as a means of expression is more significant in *space* than the face and eyes. From a distance the expression of the human face and the eyes can only be seen clearly by an infinitely small part of a theatre audience. The student will discover that when the body is, for instance, in profile and the face and the eyes are not seen—or when the actor has his back to the audience, or is upstage, or if he turns to his fellow actor—none of the expression in his eyes or his face can be seen and understood. This is particularly important in an age when people are so accustomed to close-ups of faces in films and television.
- If a student feels something very strongly, and expresses it with his face *behind* the mask, he cannot assume that his body will necessarily express what he feels—it probably will not. The mask is *not* a replacement for the face. The student must, as it were, find a way to convey the details of facial expression and the look in his eyes by other parts of his body.
- The mask helps the *body* say things which ordinary speech cannot express. Consequently, the mask strengthens the student's abil-

ity to act, in the sense that acting is *doing,* by enlarging his range of expression beyond the use of words.
- On different people, the same mask can look quite different.
- The mask changes expression in different lights. The actor must develop a kind of double concentration: he must be completely *in* what he is doing, but, at the same time, he must control his way of doing it. If he wants the audience to be convinced by what he shows them, if he wants to make them *believe* in what he does, *he* must be the first to believe in it.
- The mask reveals and rejects lies.

But in all this, the important thing is not the mask or the interesting idea, the important thing is the acting.

At first the students find this work strange. Some resent the mask because it makes them feel claustrophobic; others are frightened by it, by its magic. However, they are all impressed by the effect it has on them. Only a minority will be able to master this work quickly. Some try to oversimplify and so fall into the trap of conventional characterisation. Others take to it very strongly but they try to express with the mask what it cannot express: for instance, psychological moments, internal and intimate, which may need a text in order to come alive. In fact, one reason working with masks is good is that such work is anti-psychological.

The mask is demanding because it can only live at a certain level. To reach that level, the student needs more courage than in any other form of improvisation: the courage to try, to do, to dare, to launch himself into invention.

Acting requires the right sort of concentration. Once the student has discovered the results that can be obtained through concentration, he tends, in his improvisation, to over-concentrate and through that to become passive and constrained, in a word, constipated. He may obtain a *kind* of truth but it has no performance value.

How to discover the meeting point between the internal and the external is one of the essential secrets of acting. From the actor's discovery of the exact point of equilibrium between the internal and external comes a rich diversity.

Feeling of itself does not provide everything. If one does not feel anything, it often helps to *do* something concrete, something physical; then the feeling comes. The mind should also play its part; it does not follow that the acting will become intellectual, it may just become clearer.

Perhaps teachers and directors in the future will be able to simplify the training and come more quickly to the mask and spend more time on it. For gifted students, there might even be some kind of specialisation. However, let us remember that students usually come to acting schools to become interpretive actors; some are no good without texts. Others, good in improvisation, may come to nothing in interpretation.

Nevertheless, improvisation must be carried far enough to achieve a transposition *away from* everyday reality; the actor must be able to express the essence of the moment. This is one of the reasons why I feel it is important that students know about the Chinese and Japanese theatre, whose actors have the extraordinary ability, with a light approach, to catch concretely the essence of human gesture, action and behaviour in a most complete way without falling into stereotyped forms. Their representation of all aspects of life has reality, delicacy, and spirituality. But, of course, their students start work on the performing arts at the age of eight!

This concrete object, the mask, allows the student to work through all the problems of acting. It helps him to discover the correct balance between concentration and control and, in improvisation, it frees his body to express what he is experiencing in a way speech cannot. It increases his physical power, and, because his body is put into relief by the immobility of the mask, he can express specific things without facial expression.

Character Improvisation

> JOHN HOUSEMAN: "How do you define a comic character?"
> MICHEL SAINT-DENIS: "I don't define them—they define themselves."

Why is it so vital for a student of acting to study the techniques of comedy and farce? Because of their monumental historical and

Fourth-year students David Schramm and David Ogden Stiers in the Juilliard Drama Division's production of Moliere's *Scapin*, directed by Pierre Lefèvre.

Michel Saint-Denis as Oscar Knie.

social importance and because their techniques are more alive, more inventive, more flexible and daring than those of any other form of theatre. Because comedy and farce cover a vast area, their means of expression are marvellously varied and they encompass an inexhaustible gallery of personages, types and silhouettes. The talent for acting comedy and farce seems to me based on an actor's natural generosity of spirit, and demands vigour, boldness of invention and a vivacity and exuberance of execution that reaches a sort of physical radiance. These are, indeed, special gifts.

Comedy and farce are in direct touch with the life of the people. Farce is usually concerned with the common people, while comedy deals with the whole scale of society in all its evolutions. Comedy takes its nourishment from the ridiculous, and its themes from the vices of all social classes in all periods.

THE WAY I WORKED

The idea of using Character and Comic Improvisation, with and without masks, as an element in actor training came to me in 1924. I had invented a comic character called Oscar Knie. Jean Dasté, a fellow actor in the Compagnie des Quinze, had invented a character called César, who became the companion of Oscar. I think it might be helpful here if I start this section on Character Improvisation with a brief description of how Oscar came to life.

As it happened, I started from a costume. I had had vague notions about Oscar for a long time but I could do nothing at all until I found—among the costumes from a production of Copeau's adaptation of *The Brothers Karamazov*—an old, late-19th-century coat and a pair of mouldy, black-green, baggy trousers which were so pliable they took on the shape of every move I made.

I had a stick and also came upon an old piece of carpet, which, rolled up, gave me an air of authority which I would not have had by using gestures of my hand alone. A prop is not just a prop, nor a stick a stick: they can become, somehow, extensions of the actor and the range of transformation they are capable of is almost inexhaustible.

These four inanimate objects, the coat, trousers, carpet and stick, started my imagination working and began to give shape to my early intuitions of Oscar. This was not happening at an intellectual level; I had no "idea" about Oscar; it was more something I could feel in my bones.

This basic costume led me to observe closely the movements and gestures of a then-famous French political figure who wore clothes of a similar cut; and in La Chaux-de-Fonds, a small town in Switzerland, I also became fascinated by the night-porter of the hotel we stayed in, who was rather short and had a peculiar way of walking, standing and talking. Somehow, and I was not sure how, these encounters began to feed Oscar. There were also memories of my father and some literary influences at work: Dostoievsky and Dickens—could it have been the old man Karamazov, or Pickwick? I'm not sure. At any rate, bit by bit, I got the idea of the mask I needed and modelled it myself. From the feel of the clothes on my body, from my observation of the politician and the porter and from the mask came my inspiration. With the last minute addition of a hat, I had equipped my character from head to foot.

It was only at this moment of my work that I could go on to form, more or less intellectually, a conception of Oscar and begin to work on the practical scenarios which would finally lead me to the full realisation of this character.

Oscar was not actually born yet; the birth of a character is a very slow process. All that existed was an embryo, a silhouette. Oscar had some difficulty in speaking because, at this early stage, his existence was based primarily on physical expression. Oscar mumbled for a long time, until his silhouette began to fill out. I did not want to set anything too early. I then took Oscar into various simple scenarios, basic, everyday situations. For example, he met César for the first time. By chance, Dasté had reached the same stage in his work as I. Dasté's César was a kind of dry fish, a sort of Don Quixote, and my Oscar was to become a sort of Sancho Panza, but with much more common sense and a great deal more pessimism. Oscar hated César.

Through the sketches with Dasté, I began to discover one tiny but important personal trait of Oscar's. I had to take the greatest care not to lose this first, concrete glimmer of character. Later, another trait emerged into the foreground in sharp relief to the other spontaneous bits of Oscar's physical expression; then another and another and so on. Each time I tried these traits out in action in special situations, seeking which ones would fit into the rapidly growing character of Oscar Knie.

After all this trial and error—improvising, rehearsing successive scenes, then setting them, and not changing them, except for changes in minute details and intensity—Oscar Knie was born: naive, vain, sentimental, weak (but imperious when successful), carried to extremes, quick to anger and despair, often drunk, a great talker, full-blooded and, sometimes, obscene.

As for the invention of words, one can never be sure that the words or sentences one invents for comic improvisations will *really* have the effect on an audience one had hoped for. In one of his scenes, I remember Oscar eating a banana. While he was peeling it in an elaborate way, he was saying: "Je vais la pelurer" in a dark, serious, passionate tone. This literally means: "I am going to peel it." But there is a slight double-entendre there and the audience, sensing that, could not stop their laughter. There was such an acclamation it stopped the show. They had read into this sentence much more than I had intended.

This is obviously very difficult work to do and it needs, more than any other, faith in one's previous work and faith in one's self.

I had invented everything—the character, the acting, the text; I did not have a director out front to help me. It was at that time that it became clear to me that a difference exists between the work of the actor/improviser and that of the actor/interpreter. I realized that the process the latter follows is more complex, as he must bring to life from a text a character with the same reality as the characters an improviser creates with no text. The interpreter begins with a text, the improviser begins with himself. It might be said that a memorised text should be assimilated by the actor/interpreter in such a way that it finally comes out of him with a spontaneity comparable to that which is achieved by an actor/improviser.

Earlier I referred to this difference between the actor/interpreter and the actor/creator and noted that the theatre can encourage only a very few men and women who are specially gifted as improvisers to devote themselves entirely to it. However, I also pointed out that *all* actors must start with this creative, imaginative way of working. Character improvisation offers us the best means of developing this creative imagination in the young actor.

WAYS OF WORKING WITH STUDENTS

By this time the student will feel the need to add costume elements to his rehearsal clothes, not for their decorative effects, but in order to amplify and augment the power of his dramatic expression.

Contrary to what was done previously in the work on silent and group improvisation and with the basic masks, the student now has at his disposal cast-off clothes such as shirts, sleeves, old hats, cloaks and shoes—elements of costume from which disguises of all kinds can be made, disguises not whimsical or historical, but realistic. They become a kind of extension of the actor—as was the case with Oscar's rolled piece of carpet.

At the same time, platforms, steps and screens seem called for, as are a few pieces of furniture.

The student is encouraged to learn how to handle such musical instruments as guitars, concertinas, percussion instruments or, perhaps, even saxophones.

At the start of a class, after having chosen his mask and having observed it and worn it for a while, the student is asked to make his selection from the elements assembled from the wardrobe and prop departments.

All these tools, however, are there only to arouse and sustain the improviser's invention, to provide him with the widest possible means of expression. The essential thing is the *inventiveness* itself.

The student begins his endeavour to give life to his chosen mask-character. The character should, preferably, be a character in a contemporary situation, because a beginning acting student should not, yet, as he would usually want to do, try to reach out for a personage like Macbeth or Lear. He would not be ready for it; he would not yet know how to present emotionally and physically a person so far removed from his own experience.

The moment the student has found the embryo of this character, its outline, ways should be devised to provoke the character into speaking. Not the mere chatter of false conversation, of desperate banalities; but rather, at first, something on the order of exclamations, cries, insults, but such as might burst forth from real people, *not* from caricatures. Only farce in its freest form, at its most primitive, and often at its grossest, calls forth an inner, explosive strength substantial enough to breed a valid word. And that word cannot surge up except from the subsoil of one's being, from the blood and guts of the character. In my experience these outburts have invariably been comic.

It is the *vis-comica,* the comic life-force, existing in a comic character strongly felt by an actor, that allows the word to explode.

It is here that the teacher must, discreetly, prevent the student from inventing words or sentences that do not relate to his inner state, words that he might seek shelter behind until he has invented physical actions with the mask: the doing must come first, before the speaking.

The fact that character improvisation in its comic manifestations leads the actor to invent words, phrases and speeches should not surprise us. We know that in the tradition of the Commedia dell'Arte the actor/improviser was often a cultivated man, a man of resources, but the serious parts—the noble, the tragic, the poetic, and also the Inamorati—were always acted from a text written by dramatists attached to the troupe. This would seem to indicate that only in the case of the comic parts were the words improvised, and that invention in tragedy springs from quite different sources.

OBSERVATION AND DISCOVERY

The masks used in character improvisation are, of course, very different from the "basic" ones—the four ages of man ones. Some of them are half masks, but these will still create distinct impressions on the student. Whether full masks or half masks, they are all designed to allow his speech to be heard distinctly and to inspire the student to action.

Again, the first and most important thing is to choose the right mask. This should be done only after having tried on a number of different masks in quick succession and having gone through various actions with them. Contrary to what we have said about not looking into a mirror while wearing one of the "basic" masks, for work with half masks the mirror has, strangely enough, proved very useful.

It is a subtle point, but the student must not start his work from an idea but, rather, from inspiration. There is no one way that this happens: some students will first respond to a mask, others to a prop, still others to a piece of clothing. The student should be given the freedom to find out which point of departure is best for him; sometimes mistakes teach a great deal. One never knows what will provoke the birth of a character and nourish it.

For example, I might come upon a racquet: what is this? I have never seen anything like it? What is it? Is it to help me keep above water when swimming? Or is it a kitchen tool—a sieve perhaps? The thing itself, in this case the tennis racquet, will lead me to play with it in a certain way. Without thinking or planning anything, I let my whole physical being respond to the stimulus of the prop: a large saucepan can become a crown; a pair of scissors can be used as a lorgnette; a cigar might turn into a hypodermic syringe in the hands of a mad doctor. Chaplin made use of a transformation of this kind during a classic episode in *The Gold Rush:* his shoes became, for the starving prospector, a delicious lobster; and the shoe laces turned into the claws of the lobster from which Chaplin delicately and with great relish sucked out the meat and the juice.

Such elements must serve what the actor wants to do; they must never drown the character. What the student chooses—the shape it has and the transformation it undergoes once he starts to use it—must have a purpose associated with his initial impression of the character. But I repeat: this is in no way an intellectual process; thinking comes much later. Form enters the work only in its final stages. This first phase of the work, observation and discovery, is an active state of *doing* in which the actor tries things out. The mask or the prop or the clothing will induce in the actor a state of being-in-action, a kind of intoxication, from which a character may emerge.

We can also see that this process of observation and discovery-through-doing forces the actor to bring a prop or accessory to life, whether it be a false nose, a beard or a pair of too large or too small shoes, or even padding. In the first term, in the work on physical transformations, the student learns to act the padding

Constantin Stanislavski improvising.

Third-year students Colm Feore, Ann-Marie MacDonald and Ronald Lea in the National Theatre School of Canada's production of Ionesco's *The Bald Soprano*, directed by Derek Goldby. *(Photo: Barbra-renée Elsis.)*

without actually wearing it. Now, in this character-improvisation work, he is given real padding to experiment with. He must come to feel that it is part of his flesh and bones, not a piece of costume. A slim student may begin a simple transformation exercise on the premise: "I am a very fat woman." She is then given actions to do. Throughout the exercises she develops her transformation to such an extent that we begin to *see* her fatness. When she can do this successfully she will be in no danger of taking her real padding for granted.

In other words, we want to give the student a sense of oneness with his props and help him realise that even the inanimate object he uses is intimately related to the character and its actions.

Action with simple, everyday props and accessories can be carried to great lengths, as for instance, with smoking. Consider the way a cigarette, a cigar or a pipe is lit by:

- a conscientious smoker
- an easily distracted smoker
- a nervous character
- an exhibitionist
- a timid person
- one who can't stop laughing as he lights his cigarette

Or the endless possibilities of fiddling with eye glasses:

- There is the person who finds he can't read because his glasses are dirty; he tries to clean them, puts them on the wrong way round, then gives up and pushes them up on his head. After a while he forgets where he has put them; he tries to find them everywhere and can't. He gets angry with himself; then, grad-ually, it dawns on him that perhaps . . . they are on his head. He stops himself just before his hand touches his glasses: then he finally dares . . . and finds them. Great satisfaction.

Or observe the way people read the newspaper: the character who can never turn the pages of his newspaper properly and gets them all entangled; the short-sighted reader; the one who is con-stantly disturbed by a fly or a buzzing wasp.

There are some oral tricks which the student should master, such as:

- laughing
- sneezing
- belching
- yawning
- snoring
- hiccuping
- stuttering

or stuttering interrupted by hiccuping, or laughing and sneezing at the same time, or sneezing while desperately trying not to.

Then there are a number of physical tricks that a student with talent for farce or slapstick should practice, such as:

- slipping on a banana skin
- stumbling
- limping in various ways
- tripping
- tripping going down steps
- tripping going up steps
- both of the above ending with and then without falling down
- getting entangled in a piece of cord and trying to free oneself
- falling off a chair
- falling off a table as preparation for falling from battlements

There are many useful exercises from clown and circus schools that should be incorporated in the training as well.

Summing Up

Improvisation, in our understanding of the work, is a kind of research; it is a way of working through which the actor's experiences pass to nourish his imagination; through improvisation these experiences can be made to serve his interpretation of a text and enable him to present a visible, complete reality.

We want the student to see that, left entirely to himself, without the help of a playwright or a director, he can, with his body and his imagination, create and present a full dramatic life. Through improvisation an actor will be able to see that he can be not only an interpreter but also a creator.

We have always considered the work on improvisation to be central to the formation of an actor.

It is during this work that the chemistry develops between the student's various sensibilities and the inner existence and the physical reality of the personage he will have to present. This chemical reaction will impel him to action.

Improvisation develops the faculties of invention, imagination and concentration and at the same time gives the actor a sense of freedom.

To me, the basic, essential responsibility for creating a role rests with the actor. If we are able to train accomplished actors who can bring to their acting an initiative and a sense of responsibility, this, no doubt, will be due to their experiences with improvisation.

Chapter Seven

INTERPRETATION

Theory should crown experience, not precede it.

IT IS DIFFICULT TO explain how the transition from improvisation to interpretation takes place, but many actors must have felt, as I myself have, the satisfaction, in improvisation, of giving totally of oneself, mentally and physically. Indeed, when one begins interpretative work and is separated from improvisation, there grows within oneself a feeling for a paradise lost. One does not feel it immediately; it is only while coping with the difficulties of interpretation that the memory of the liberty one felt when improvising returns.

What makes the transition from improvisation to interpretation so difficult is that the student, from the beginning of his improvisational work, has been going through the experience of acting without words. He has learned to compose a character and give physical expression to what he has felt and conceived through that inner chemistry we have mentioned before. But in all this work he was deprived of a written text and only from time to time was he permitted to use words spontaneously invented by himself. But in interpretation, on the contrary, the student must submit to somebody else's text, the meaning of which, the psychology and sequence of action—the "mise-en-action"—emerge out of a collaboration between the actor and the director. It is only through an active submission to the text, intelligently understood, that the student can gradually regain that lost-paradise feeling of the improvisation phase of his work when everything depended on him. In order to do this in his interpretative work he must master the text. Because there will always be the risk that an actor may impose his own invention instead of submitting to that of the author, we must be sure that the actor's sensitivity is open to the *text* and not to his own subjective inner feelings or his own subjective emotional reactions. He must make himself at ease with the text—even better, become inspired by it. But how is he to extract its meaning; how is he to become sensitive to the inspiration given by style? How is he to create the reality of a personage—and that personage's relationships to others—and thus make the play come alive?

To my mind there is no question about the inspiration that can be given by style. Style is an instrument whose intelligent and sensitive use must lead to what is the most secret, the most essential quality of what the author has to say.

But it is also true that even with the greatest authors it sometimes happens that the meaning of certain passages is not completely penetrable and therefore is difficult for the student and the director to understand. One must not rush to find, much less impose, a meaning; to do so can have quite serious consequences. Meaning may clarify itself only after many readings of a specific passage within the context of the whole play.

This then is a crucial point: when we say *inspired* by a text, we do *not* mean that one should analyse it, that one should attempt to define all its psychological sources, and we certainly do not mean that one should explain it.

The student/actor must, ultimately, give a text as much *reality* as he would if it had been invented by himself, as if it were the text of the character he has created. At the same time, the student and his director must take great care not to reduce that text to their own subjectivity and so impose themselves on it; the author is greater than they are. They must therefore let *him* speak, and they must submit to him, not passively, but with a sort of sympathy, a communion, with what is most secret in the author.

It is also true that in encountering a text, a student will almost always find its style disorientating, bewildering—that is, if there is a *true* style there.

It is not possible to enter into this communion with a great play without the constant practice of texts and without a sort of vital spirit of the tongue, a vital revelation in sound.

If considered in an objective way, the author's text, the personages and the situations which emerge, will offer an invitation, for the actor and the director, to go beyond themselves.

The heroism of Corneille, the sensitivity of Racine, the charity of Chekhov's observations—so intimately bound to his characters—all these risk being distorted if approached by the student or director with a subjective attitude.

It is as difficult to approach a text by T. S. Eliot, Beckett, Ionesco or Pinter—to know what it means and to espouse the style in which it is written—as it is to approach a text by Shakespeare, Marlowe, Molière or Ben Jonson.

There will always be in a great author a poetic, human expression which one is totally unable to analyse or explain completely. But there will be no reality, no human or artistic value, unless the meaning reaches the audience at the same time as "la figure du language"—the face of the language.

Many interpretations, although perfectly faithful, are often empty and flat. This would not be so if the student/actor would read the play, not with his head, but in that perceptive way which gives an understanding well beyond simple comprehension.

All this is exactly why the passage from improvisation to interpretation is so difficult: at the end of the student's improvisational work—his first year—he is capable of a far more striking *physical* expression than he can yet manage in interpretation. Of course, this does not apply to that minority of students who are particularly gifted, and whose work will flower with a text rather than in improvisation.

The text is obviously the vehicle of interpretation. From this point of view, the roots of interpretation are in the preparatory work on speech and texts done in the first year of the student's training: the Non-Dramatic Readings, culminating in Poetry (l'Expression Parlée) and in Play Readings.

During the early rehearsal periods, it is very difficult to convince an actor that he has to restrain himself from running before he can walk; this is particularly so in working on the great classical plays. In a classical play the actor must not hurry or jump upon the character. He must not enslave the text by a premature conception of the character. Psychological and emotional understanding of a character should come through familiarity with the text, not from outside it. The actor must know how to wait, how to refuse, so as to remain free. He must be like a glove, open and flexible, but flat. Then, by degrees, the text, the imagination, the associations aroused by the text penetrate and bring the actor to life. Ways are prepared for the character to creep in slowly and animate the glove—the glove which is the actor—with his blood, his nerves, with his breathing system, his voice, with the light of his own lucid control switching on and off. The whole complex "machinery" is at work; it has been put into action by the text.

I once saw a naturalistic play where the actors applied strictly the teachings of the "Method": they were not concerned so much with the presentation of the play, the "cloth," as with the "lining." Their faces, their gestures and words, were far less important to them than their nervous systems, their secret "stirrings," the meaning behind the words. Though a photograph of life was intended, only the negative was being shown, not the finished print.

Our feeling is that the student, in his acting, should *present* rather than *impersonate* and should give first place to objective gesture rather than to the study of subjective psychology.

REHEARSAL TECHNIQUES

Acting cannot be taught, technique can.

In the first two years, work in interpretation is done essentially through the process of rehearsing: the student will learn to act by rehearsing plays, by going through experiences that gradually teach him to *act* with a text.

It was in the class in Silent Improvisation that the student, starting from himself, discovered and explored acting—doing. In the work in Rehearsal Techniques he has to start from the text of a play—from something *outside* himself. The interaction between improvisation and interpretation will soon become apparent: the first is there to animate the second. The whole of our training is divided between improvisation (the creative part of an actor's work) and interpretation—the two main lines of the life work of an actor. This is in order to arrive at a *visual* vitality, and it is why we give improvisation such an importance in the first year, an importance over all the other disciplines. It prepares the student for the transition from the rest of the technical disciplines to the improvisational work, that is, from technique to invention.

The use of improvisation as part of the Rehearsal Techniques training is nowadays an accepted way of working. But if improvisation is to be used in conjunction with the rehearsal of a particular play, it should not be introduced until the play has been read in its entirety and the first "shock" of it has struck the student. Then the play should be read again.

After the second reading, silent physical, and, later, verbal improvisation may be useful, as it may become a lead to the interpretation of a role. But the student must choose for his improvisation a character in a situation from the play. It should not be just any kind of improvisation, but a sort of testing of different ways of *doing* which may enlighten the student as to the character's inner life. All this must be well planned and based on the knowledge of what the role and the situations of the play demand.

I have sometimes seen rehearsal improvisations done by actors who were not really familiar enough with the play and this has, of course, its hazards as it can lead the actor away from the role. This danger, inherent in all rehearsal improvisations, is far more serious in verbal improvisations, where it can estrange the student from the text from which everything stems.

As for verbal improvisations, they are relatively easy to do in a realistic style, but if they are tried, for instance, with one of Chekhov's plays, the student will find that his own necessarily colloquial improvisations cannot approach the inner life of Chekhov's characters, let alone come near Chekhov's seemingly simple language. The student will think that Chekhov's language is straightforward, easy to learn and speak—but, in fact, its poetic realism and its special, personal rhythm comes through only when spoken by an actor who has the voice and speech techniques to play with the lines, to modulate his tones, and thus to capture the meaning behind the words. This poetic level the student will not be able to reach. Realistic improvisations will spoil his feelings—and his ear—for the peculiar finesse of Chekhov's style: Chekhov's poetic realism leads, through an indirectness of language, to a kind of visionary expression, which is not easy to capture.

If the student has only a scanty knowledge of a text, he will be inclined through his verbal improvisations to fabricate meaning and, when coming back to the text, try to fit it to those fabrications.

It may also lead him to a subjective, erroneous psychology; it is not important to find out what a character *thinks*, but what a character thinks in a *situation* related to the play.

As to the classics—Shakespeare for one—it is very hard to make up words for a character with the stature of Lear and not to lose entirely the grandiose, poetic structure of his language. And, too, how will a student be able to assimilate the background of life and feelings of a man like Lear from the text alone, without first having studied the whole of Shakespeare's time?

Acting, physical and verbal, must be charged with meaning and never be a mere illustration of life. To avoid a stale interpretation of a formal written text, one must start from the *text;* psychology cannot surreptitiously be slipped behind real poetry—but it very often flows out of it.

Of course classical plays present us with many passages which seem dead or empty; beauty of form has prevailed over matter. If those passages are not cut, then a sort of virtuosity is required of the actor, a special ability to make what is formal and shallow appear credible and attractive.

As far as the young student is concerned, he must realise that he cannot interpret works of the past in terms of the language and styles of today. He must assimilate the *reality*, the life of past styles. There are no two worlds; there is not a world of modern and a world of classic theatre. There is only one theatre, as there is only one world. But there is a continuity which slowly changes and develops from ancient to modern styles.

The traditional heritage of the world now belongs to the *whole* world, where cultures intermingle so freely that, in addition to contemporary texts of a more or less realistic nature in one's own language, one is obliged to interpret works of the past in translation. We have to subject these translations to the same subtle, lucid examination which we would give a work written in our own language. Translations too often corrupt style or, in any case, modify its nature.

Style, from whichever epoch, consists of form and content, the two being inseparable. Style is the opposite of mannerism, of pretense, of artifice; it is the visible mark of the artist and the sign of his originality. Style reveals the very soul of a genuine work.

In order to feel the very heartbeat of a work, the student/actor has to know how to decipher and understand a text that may feel strange "on the tongue;" he will have to discover the text's tone and tempo, mine its inner richness and learn how to speak the text with ease.

The musician of today, when confronted with a classical piece of music, finds in its score all kinds of specific signs—notes, indications of tempo, colour and sentiment. But in a play the student has to find all this by himself with no indicative signs from the author.

I would like to clarify what I mean by the terms classical, naturalism, and realism.

By *classical* I mean the long tradition that began with Greek tragedy and comedy and was developed to its fullest extent in the 16th and 17th centuries by Shakespeare and others in England and by French dramatists in the 17th and 18th centuries.

By *realism* I mean all that is attached to the school which began with Ibsen and Strindberg and such German and Austrian authors as Wedekind, Buechner and Schnitzler; with the Russians Gorky, Chekhov and Ostrovsky; with the Irish Sean O'Casey and the American Eugene O'Neill.

These styles need not be opposed to each other—they simply co-exist.

It is important to realise that there are two kinds of realism: there is, on the one hand, the deep realism which studies and expresses the nature of things, the meaning of human life, what happens behind appearances; and, on the other, the realism which is satisfied with the representation of the external. This superficial realism was called at the beginning of the present century *naturalism*. Here I would like to make a distinction between realism, which applies to the art of all times, and naturalism which is an ephemeral form of art, belonging to the period of Zola and Antoine or Theodore Dreiser.

The reader will begin to understand that what I strongly advocate for our training is a blending of classicism and realism.

The Reading of Plays

In the beginning of the second term, after he has experienced Non-Dramatic Readings, the student will be confronted with Dramatic Readings, in which he reads actual plays. The reason why this class in the reading of dramatic texts is part of the Rehearsal Techniques course is to introduce the student to striking examples of differences in style in the writing of plays and (later in his training) to make him aware of differences in style in the acting of them.

At this point, no demands are made on the student's technique of voice, diction or interpretation. Nor is he asked to analyse character or situations. He should have a general perception rather than a complete understanding of the play.

For the purpose of maintaining unity throughout the four-year course, we have chosen, in all the various stages of the training, to concentrate on three specific categories of plays: classical tragedy, classical comedy and realism in all its forms.

The three play readings should follow one another at the closest possible intervals and each should not last longer than two and a half weeks at the most. The teacher/directors guiding these readings should preferably be those who worked with the same group of students in the previous term on the Non-Dramatic Readings, so that there is a certain continuity in the climate already established by teacher and student.

The teacher should point out that although in the Non-Dramatic Readings the student had a certain freedom in the way he read, in the Play Readings this freedom cannot be used in the same way, as he is now working with texts written in a given form.

The teacher should give a short talk before the reading begins, in order to familiarise the student with the life and times of the author and the whole background of the play. This should encourage the student to explore the epoch for himself and to read other plays of the period.

In order not to separate the readings completely from doing, the director should stop from time to time and ask questions, such as: "What is happening here? What is the situation?" These questions are asked in order to establish facts, not to analyse them. Or the director might say: "Tell me briefly in your own words what you have just read." And after that: "Try to act, to improvise without words, what you just read and told us."

It is, of course, important to choose situations from the play that lend themselves to silent improvisations of that kind.

After these interruptions the reading of the play should be continued.

Constantly changing the approach to these readings should be exhilarating. This will make them more alive and non-academic and will help do away with that reverential awe which college students, especially, sometimes have for classical texts.

The order in which these plays should be read can be varied. One could start with a tragedy by Shakespeare, then read a Greek comedy and finish with a realistic play; or one could start with a realistic play and then go on to a classical comedy and end the play readings with a Shakespeare tragedy or another classical play of the same calibre.

I have tried various ways myself but finally found it preferable to end the play readings with a Shakespeare play. Since this last play is the first which we rehearse in a precise way—the other two are only read—it is important that it be in the style furthest away from the student's experience, the style that will force him to go beyond his capabilities of the moment.

There are other ways of bringing home to the student the notion of style. I suppose one could begin by exploring the variety of styles in realistic playwriting: the differences between Chekhov, Ibsen, Pirandello and Pinter. But the differences between those authors are much less striking than those the student will perceive between a Shakespeare play, a Greek comedy and a twentieth-century realistic play.

As I have said earlier in this book, I strongly believe in blending classicism and realism in the training of the actor. So, however helpful the early study of realism might be in the work on interpretation, it would be, I think, ill-advised to put too much emphasis on it *before* attacking the other styles. In spite of all its apparent advantages, there is a danger in pushing realism too far too early: it restrains, it hinders the work of interpreting the great classics, and, therefore, impoverishes the craft of the actor, rather than enriching it.

Through experience we have found that work in the Rehearsal Techniques course progresses best if scheduled in a certain manner. A description of this schedule, indicating the time slots of the three plays the student is going to rehearse during each year, is presented on the following pages.

THE FIRST YEAR—The Discovery Year

The Discovery Play

At the beginning of the first term the student is put through an early and, necessarily, limited experience of acting. He works on a classical play (Shakespeare or one of similar scope) without yet possessing sufficient technical means of expression.

It is like throwing someone into deep water to make him discover what he can do to keep himself afloat. We call this project the Discovery Play Project. Through it, the student can test himself by going through every phase of the rehearsal of a play under real conditions. This gives him some idea of the extent of his technical equipment, of what he has and of what he lacks; and by the end of these rehearsals, which last about four weeks but no more, the student will have discovered by himself some of the problems facing him and the gap that exists between the demands that a text makes on him and his ability, both technically and imaginatively, to meet those demands.

The experience gained during this rehearsal period usually shocks the student into a realisation of how essential the training of the voice and body is to his development as an actor; this will make him much more responsive to the training.

The Discovery Play offers the faculty a picture of the particular needs, the shortcomings, of each student. This will allow them to plan the geography of the student's future training.

In the course of the Discovery Play rehearsals, the play is taken from its first readings through a series of run-throughs. The first complete reading should be done in as relaxed a manner as possible, without the student attempting to establish any emotional involvement with the play.

The director must create a climate in which he can guide the student rather than direct him. He should not impose any ideas about interpretation, and he must prevent the student from going too deeply, too soon, into interpretation. He should not allow him to prematurely set ideas about voice, gesture or character.

The director should stop the student's attempts at interpretation if he feels that the effort is too much for the technical equipment the student has at the moment. They can go on to the next scene and return to the troublesome one later, when the student may feel more detached and able to let the play "come" to him, gradually. It is important never to push or force an interpretation out of a desire to achieve an effect.

The students should read the play several times with the director, who may stop now and then to help them in their comprehension of the play by clarifying its general sense. But he should not, at this stage, go too far into explanations. He should ask occasional questions about the meaning of certain key passages and scenes, in order to encourage the student to find out things for himself. The director should help the student to understand the relationships between the various characters; he should touch on the differences in rhythm between the verse and prose passages, without expecting the student to cope with these differences. He merely makes the student aware that such textual variety exists.

In the second phase of these rehearsals the play should be staged *lightly:* the student should be given simple, meaningful moves; the director should explain that within the stage action the student must make these moves his own, without, however, taking too many liberties that would destroy the orchestration of the whole.

The student should also be made aware of the movement of the other characters around him, and how these affect both him and them. He must understand the limits of individual freedom.

This way of working on the Discovery Play makes it all very slow to begin with and will require much patience from teacher and student.

All students concerned with the play must be present at all rehearsals—this is essential, since each will benefit greatly from what is said to the others. Seeing others' mistakes as well as one's own is a valuable form of learning.

The faculty should never make the student feel that he is being watched and judged during the early stages of these rehearsals; they should start dropping in, casually, after the actors are on their feet.

During the last week of rehearsals, at whatever stage the play is in, it should be seen by the entire faculty.

Although the play will be shown in one of the rehearsal rooms, by then that room will have established itself as a stage for most of the students. On the day of the showing the students will act as best they can, up to, and sometimes beyond, their limits.

This session should in no way be treated as a performance, but as one of the rehearsals. In the beginning of the training we call any performance the students give a showing, and not a performance. The reason is that we want to encourage the student's concentration, and leave him free to make, with guidance, the connection between his inner existence and his means of expression, without disturbing him with the feeling that he has to prove himself.

The important thing in the first year is to plant the roots of the actor's invention at the deepest possible level.

Alongside these first rehearsal sessions, the technical work on voice and body, early speech practice and classes in the Alexander Technique take place. Improvisation classes are added halfway through the Discovery Play rehearsals.

Classes usually take place in the morning, while the afternoon is given over to the rehearsal sessions of the Discovery Play; this arrangement allows the student to concentrate entirely on the play. It is absolutely essential not to overload the student with too many different disciplines at the beginning of his training; he will be inclined to apply things learned in his technical classes to the rehearsals and so lose the uncluttered, spontaneous approach to this work. It is only when this spontaneity is maintained that the student has a real opportunity to test himself; he will gain considerably by doing so.

We have found, over many years, that the Discovery Play is an invaluable and enlightening experience for students and teachers alike and sets the tone for the rest of the training. It is a demonstration of how one gains knowledge of the actor's craft through experience rather than through thinking.

THE CRITIQUE

A forbidding and often misleading necessity, criticism should be handled carefully at this early stage of the training. There are many different kinds, many different degrees of criticism. The Head of the school and the faculty should decide what can be said to each student and by whom, as well as what is better left for a later stage when the student will be more able to understand it.

Students are particularly vulnerable at this critical point of their training. They certainly do not know enough about themselves yet: they are either too sure of themselves or in complete despair. But on the other hand, the student must learn throughout the training to take criticism from others and also to sharpen his own sense of self-criticism.

The faculty must judge not his "performance" of this first play, the Discovery Play, but the student's artistic potentiality, his present equipment and his attitude towards the work.

After the showing of the Discovery Play, there is a general meeting of the faculty and all the students in the play. Much depends on the right handling of this first meeting with the students at which their work is discussed; it is a testing ground for both students *and* teachers and it is here that a mutual trust may—or may not—begin to be established.

The Head of the school should be the first to speak. He should give, in broad outline, his general impression of the showing. The director of the play then talks to each student, occasionally asking, if he wishes, one or another of the teachers to comment on certain technical aspects of the student's work.

After this general meeting, it is useful to have another session with the director and students, without other members of the faculty being present, so that the students can ask questions about comments made at the general meeting. This is important, as many things that trouble students in the beginning can be aired and be given considerate answers. A period of time should then be set aside to work on certain scenes from the play so that the students can try to understand in action the points made at the critique, check the criticism for themselves and make whatever adjustments are necessary.

General *theoretical* questions about acting should be avoided; experience is more helpful to a student than theories.

This is an invaluable preparation for subsequent stages of the training; later, the student will remember these first rehearsal difficulties and this will help him to measure his own progress.

It is during these first weeks that the defects of each student should be detected and appropriate remedies considered.

The seeds of our training are planted during this first term and much depends on this in the student's later years.

THE CHALLENGE

> In every meeting with students *they* are the real directors at work—all instruction, all disciplines, all exercises center on them.

The period of the Discovery Play has ended and the first general critique has been held. All work on interpretation as such is temporarily suspended until towards the middle of the second term of the first year. This is done in order to prevent the student from acting a role before he is capable of interpreting it. He must first discover what *acting* means before trying to use a text again. Supported by the technique he is acquiring and working from his own inner life and creative imagination, he must gain sufficient experience and understanding to enable him later to interpret dramatic texts without excess or affectation. The experience of the Discovery Play is a means of verifying the qualities the student has, as well as a means of demonstrating to him the extent of his ability to deal with the practical difficulties encountered.

Sometimes a student has difficulty in presenting a character honestly within the spirit and atmosphere of a scene because he feels that his own inner truth is not in accord with the style of the play and that he cannot make it so. It is difficult then for him not to launch into the scene by hastily filling himself with emotion to such an extent that he no longer knows what he is doing; at such times one becomes as if slightly drunk.

After all, the difficulties of the first rehearsals are many, and all of them descend on the student at once: to speak and move at the same time, to know what to do when one has nothing to say; to make oneself heard without feeling that one is forcing and, therefore, losing the truth of what one is saying; to know how to look at one's fellow actors, or at the audience or simply at the stage, while continuing to believe in what one is doing.

How is the student to learn not to listen to himself speaking the text, not to exaggerate his voice and gestures until he becomes simply an empty form?

The student must have felt all this during the rehearsals of the Discovery Play—he must have sensed a number of things that were taking place inside him, a mélange of impulses and feelings difficult to clarify either to himself or to his audience. He must also have discovered how lost, how empty and how self-conscious an actor can feel.

This experience will have made it clear to the student that an actor has to understand and to imagine but, above all, he has to *express* his understanding and his imagination: he has to have a body and a voice which obey his every intention. And all this on a stage where everything has to be somewhat larger than life.

A musician learns to read music, appreciate the rhythm and the mood of the piece and then play it on an instrument, say a flute or a violin. He, of course, is helped by a conductor as the actor is by a director. But an actor's text is written in a notation much less precise than a musician's. The actor's music is the text—a text which he must understand and appreciate, not as a scholar, but as an artist who has to bring it to life.

The main difference is that the actor is his own flute or violin. The technical exercises the musician has to do on his chosen instrument, the actor has to do on himself. He will have to train his body so that it becomes entirely expressive from head to toe; his voice, so that it becomes supple enough to express all the nuances of feeling. The actor's movement and gestures, the flow of dramatic feeling passing through him must be supported by the actor's dramatic imagination if it is to have meaning and be clearly perceptible to an audience. The actor must know how to connect his invention to his expression. Everything he does has to be more clearly defined than in real life.

The student will begin to understand that to obtain true acting, or sincerity in acting, it is not sufficient to "feel" a character or a situation, or to be "exalted" by the dramatic or poetic value of a play.

It is not enough to understand with one's intelligence what the dramatist intended or what one should aim at to fulfill the dramatist's intention. Strong feeling and clear understanding only help if put at the service of that mysterious power to grasp and present life which a true actor has. This mysterious power can only achieve a measure of success if the actor's technical equipment is strong. An actor who knows by intuition how a part should be acted can be completely thwarted by an uncooperative body, leg, arm or face; or by a voice that is unable to shape his intuitive impulses.

What, then, is it that happens to a young student during his experience of the Discovery Play? How does he cope with establishing a character, without having technique to fall back on?

After reading a play and beginning to study it with the director, the student will find that, gradually, inside him, the image of the character forms of itself. This image grows more and more precise during the early rehearsals while the student learns and memorises the moves given to him by his director and while he familiarises himself with the text. After a while the student, in his mind's eye, sees the character move, hears him speak and he will try, as he continues the rehearsals, to reach, to bring to life, this image which has formed inside himself. But then the whole question is: how to "behave" vis-à-vis this image? When the meaning and the style of the play are close to his everyday life, or when a character is *like* the student and within the sphere of his experience of life, the acting problems are relatively easy to solve.

But if he is confronted with *King Lear*, he is placed face to face with the most difficult, the greatest challenge the theatre can present: how to find the reality of a character and a situation in a style so far removed from us as that of a Shakespearean play. Somehow the student will have to find a way of lifting himself to the imaginative sphere of characters like Lear, Goneril, Regan, whose human experience touches the extremes of cruelty, sensuality, frustrating humiliation, suffering and madness. At the same time, the actor must grasp the meaning and the beauty of their poetic language.

In any style that an actor has to interpret, he must give reality to his character and make the audience believe in this reality. But there will always be in the student a conflict between his feeling of sincerity and his sense of the reality of a play: a fight between "truth" and "style." The student comes up against these problems immediately on the first reading of a play; he must be ready to solve them.

We believe that, once the student begins to feel at home with the masterpieces of the past, the way is open to him, naturally and directly, to interpret the modern repertory of realism in all its forms. The deeper modern realism becomes, in its expression as well as in its subject matter, the more it requires actors trained in the classical disciplines to penetrate to the depth of that realism. They will then be equipped with sharper instruments than those without such training.

THE CONFLICT

> The actor must make himself available to the role
> he plays and be possessed by it.

There are many kinds of acting techniques: there is technical acting with full control of all its components; imitative acting with a model constantly before the mind's eye; and balanced acting with the right mixture of control and possession.

It is interesting to observe the fight between the personality of an actor and the character he has to present. How is the actor to deal with this—how can he make his personality and the character meet? How, indeed, is the director to deal with this? It seems to me that there is only one way and that is to be aware of this conflict, to respect it, and to learn how best it can be used to serve the play.

But some actors do not concern themselves with all this; they say "*I* am the character" or "The character is like me." They speak the text with their "own" voice and end up imposing themselves completely on the role.

There are other actors who says to themselves "I see this character. . . . I could draw him . . . I can hear him speak; he has a dark voice. . . ." This image gets more and more precise but it stays outside the actor. He makes every effort to imitate this image he has created for himself, but he cannot help but do so coldly and technically. Paradoxically, in attempting to create something different from himself, he ends up by utilising only what he *is*.

Then there is the actor who has a precise conception of the character—the actor who *lives* the character and hears him, but who does everything possible to keep himself in the background. Such an actor uses all his technical ability to prepare his inner self so that the character can possess him and animate him. This is the actor who *wants* to feel possessed by what he is acting but, at the same time, maintains control over that which possesses him. This actor believes that the character must live inside him but that he must keep watch over the direction in which his acting is taking the character; he allows his inspiration to animate his acting from the inside. It is his technique, however, which enables him to be free, to be inspired—to be possessed and controlled at the same time. There must be great invention *and* great technique, but technique must not be seen.

Second Rehearsal Project

We are in the middle of the second term of the Discovery Year, as described on page 86 in this book. For our second Rehearsal Project, we use the last play read in the Play Reading course.

Here we begin to teach in more detail the process of rehearsing a play: reading the play, breaking it down into scenes, attempting to find the key moment in each scene and exploring the relationships between characters. The emphasis then should be on giving the actors their moves—that is to say, on assigning to each actor suitable positions and moves determined by the text, its situation and action; in short, the general geography of the play. At this early stage of his training, it should not be left to the student/actor to make his own choices, as he does not yet have an overall view of the play as seen by the audience. The director does.

But placing should not be thought of as something imposed by the director. If it is considered to be a series of suggestions, something provisional, the student will not feel imprisoned by the director's proposals, but will learn to collaborate with him.

The director will show the student what is meant by "placing," how moves grow organically from the demands of the text, how the moves must be made at the right moment, in the right direction in space, in relationship to the student's fellow actors. He will also explain to the actors that the positions and moves he has given them are not absolutely final, that they may change slightly in the course of rehearsals and some may even be replaced by others. The main object here is to orchestrate the moves of a group of people so that they do not have to grope about for them, while stumbling over each other. The actors must, however, find ways to make these positions and moves their own. Once they get this out of the way, it will free them to face the real problems of acting.

There are many ways of staging: there is the method where the director just sketches the movement and does not insist on the suggested move if the actor finds it difficult to make it his own. This way of staging is particularly recommended for a Shakespeare play, because the form of the verse and the words themselves reveal the reality of the characters and situations.

But in a Chekhov play, for instance, the places and moves will have to be precise and more closely adhered to, because the meaning of the text often lies beneath the surface, and, although the words are relatively easy to memorise, to discover the meaning is not. Therefore, the actors should become familiar with the moves early on in the rehearsals.

Some directors like their actors to find their own moves, although the director may change them in order to make them more coherent.

In the early training I recommend using the way of precise placing I have described for the Discovery Play, as it is the least distracting for the student.

But whatever method is chosen, the actor will have to make the moves his own. The real problem is how to make the moves agree with the spoken text.

The director should take into consideration the state of the technical equipment the student is gradually acquiring and make his demands on the student accordingly. Through feedback from the student's technical work, the director can recognise when the student can be encouraged to break through his limitations of the moment.

It should be explained to the student that he will probably not be able to apply immediately what he has learned but that the techniques he is acquiring will, finally, lead him to a kind of liberty which he has probably already felt in his improvisational work but which will take considerably longer to experience in his work in interpretation.

This Rehearsal Project (the second in the Discovery Year) should not take more than three hours a day, five days a week, for a period not longer than four to five weeks. The reason for this is that the rest of the training—the technical training—must have time to catch up with the growing demands made on the student in the course of the Rehearsal Projects.

For the second project it may be sufficient to put on only one act of a play—after having read the whole play. The student should gradually be taught how to memorise the text *during* rehearsals, rather than alone at home, so that the life of the text can grow organically as the characters emerge. Parrot-like memorizing of a text should be discouraged. The play should be taken only through a first runthrough, book in hand if needed.

Except for absolutely essential elements, there should be only indications of a set and costumes. There should be no props—the student should be able to indicate them by now. This bareness is a great help in learning to act—to *do*.

For this project, the students do *not* work toward a performance. They do not have to achieve the play. The faculty sees the later stages of the rehearsal work and the runthrough, but the rest of the school is not invited to the showings. However, if the first-year group is divided into two divisions, working with two different directors, each division should see the other's play.

This particular way of proceeding eases many tensions. Students in their first year are preoccupied with and worried about many aspects of the training that they have not yet fully understood and absorbed. After the critique session, it is often helpful if they are left to sort out their problems on their own; if they want to, the students can always consult their teachers.

GENERAL CONSIDERATIONS

During the four-year course, the choice of plays for each group's rehearsal projects is linked, as much as possible, to the work in the other branches of the training. For instance, if we decide to use for the second project a realistic, more or less contemporary play, the teacher/director during rehearsals would constantly refer to the work in silent improvisation where, in the beginning, most exercises are based on everyday actions from the student's own immediate experience of life. If, however, the project is a Shakespeare tragedy, we have as yet little to hark back to, at this stage of the training, and can use the project only to introduce the student to the relationship between the text and the moves.

Third Rehearsal Project

The third Rehearsal Project falls into the last term of the Discovery Year and the play chosen should be linked to the work with basic masks, which begins at this time and which, in most cases, liberates the student's physical expression, extending it beyond the range of everyday life. Plays like *Noah*, *Camino Real* and *The Skin of Our Teeth*, are useful vehicles for this project.

In this term, plays should be given several showings. Although there are sound and music cues, still, only absolutely necessary elements of scenery, props and costumes should be used.

During this phase of Rehearsal Techniques, the teacher/director should draw attention to the need to time gestures and moves to the text, to the way in which a gesture or a move can underline a thought or contradict it. Some exercises should be invented to demonstrate this.

The student should be encouraged to maintain an open approach to the play; he should observe his sensations as his first impressions begin to work on him and he should put them to the test and explore many different paths before attempting to set anything. If this is done he will be able to express these discoveries clearly and in great detail. This way of proceeding will later enable him to recognize the best approach to acting a given play.

The director should also help the student to become aware of his own emotional processes and help him accomplish the transition from his own inner existence to one of wider dimensions.

By the end of this first year the student will have experienced some of the different approaches to style, without yet being able to do justice to them in his acting.

It is not always easy for either the student or the teacher to realise the extent of what the student has experienced in the course of his training. He may have some idea of what it has meant to him, but often he is not consciously aware of what he has accepted, what he has resisted and rejected or what has unconsciously stimulated him.

THE SECOND YEAR—The Transformation Year

By the second year the student should have acquired some basic experience in acting, so the plays chosen can increase in complexity and the rehearsals can now go deeper.

The first play of this year should be a realistic one; it will reinforce the skills the student was beginning to acquire before his long summer holiday began. *The Enemy of the People* and *The Lower*

Depths might be useful choices. In preparing for this play, the student will be asked to do research into the mode of living—the life and manners—of another country, one not his own, although it need not be farther removed in time than the recent past.

Work with character masks begins at this point and, as a result, greater demands regarding characterisation can now be made on the student.

At this time in the Poetry classes work begins on classical scenes and the great Shakespearian speeches. In this way the student is preparing for the next play, which should be one by Shakespeare.

This second play in the Transformation Year is a difficult one for the student to do and for the director to direct. The student's recently achieved confidence in his acting is likely to be shaken by the difficulties he now encounters, while the teacher/director must exercise patience as he watches his student struggle with the demands of a Shakespearian text. The objective here is for the student to discover how the verse embodies the heightened passion of human beings without necessarily losing the reality of those human beings.

If the student's acting seems, in some ways, to regress during this Shakespeare project, one should not worry too much. Coping with a classical text requires great attention and dealing with many new factors all at once is a formidable challenge.

One of the difficult things for the student to do at this stage is to communicate truthfully with his fellow actors *and* his audience in what is not his everyday, normal speech, but which, nevertheless, must become normal, without destroying the form of the poetry.

Again, the audience for this second project consists of only the faculty and other students.

Comedy and Farce

We now introduce a class that deals specifically with comedy and farce techniques, with the accent on comic physical action, rather than on verbal wit. This class comes at a crucial point in the student's training, forcing him to become more daring in his transformation work, obliging him to become more and more removed from himself.

After four or five weeks of these classes, the student should rehearse a short comedy or farce, so that he can apply his newly-acquired comic techniques.

This project is seen by the faculty and all the students.

In the last term of the Transformation Year a Chekhov play, or another similar Russian play, should be done. I have always found that working with such plays—particularly Chekhov's—develops in the student a deeper understanding of humanity. In a curious way, the text in Chekhov is an unimportant result of something else that is going on; it is the actor's and the director's job to find out what that something else is.

The Russian project allows the student, who by now has gone through two years of training, to utilise in a more subtle way his growing technique. Coming as it does before the summer holidays, this Russian project should give the student much food for thought for the long summer months.

By the end of his second year, the student will have encountered six plays of varied styles.

The teacher/director should be reminded that second-year rehearsals are still primarily *teaching* projects and the play is to be seen only by faculty and the other students, except the last two projects. Second-year students are still grappling with the problem of how to include an audience in their awareness without losing their concentration. This is much easier to accomplish when one is performing before an audience of familiar faces.

THE THIRD YEAR—The Interpretation Year

The work in the third year is mainly concentrated on interpretation and showings. It is still a learning year: classes in voice and speech continue, and some improvisational projects, which are more experimental in nature, might be done. The reading of plays in many contrasting styles should be taken up again.

The entire thrust of the third year is on bringing together all the elements of the training within the framework of several very detailed, highly concentrated productions, performed for invited audiences in the school's theatre.

Detailed work to improve the student's sense of timing, his projection and the musical quality of his delivery should go on. It cannot be stressed too much that it is not enough to be heard: an actor's voice has to translate the shape of a text and its tempo into meaningful sound and to convey its subtle modulations of meaning and feeling.

The first play in the third year should be a classical play, one that presents to the student a difficult text with heightened emotional situations. A play of the Jacobean period would serve very well.

The second play should be a contemporary play, perhaps a foreign one.

After that, a brief performance tour of schools and colleges should be arranged using a full-length play or several one-act plays; an experimental show with masks, music and dancing might also be useful. During this tour the students will begin to learn how to deal with different kinds of audiences. They will learn how to time their acting to the laughter of the audience, how to react to boisterous audiences of children and how to play truthfully to them. They will also learn, as they repeat their performance day after day, not to *copy* what they have done before, but to *renew* themselves and, without changing anything, act as if they had spontaneously invented everything, even the text, at the very moment of performance.

The last play of the third year should be a Restoration comedy. This style is often difficult for students to cope with. They will be better able to express the period's *physical* wit than its *verbal* wit, but an experienced director will be able to help them plunge ahead as they did during their work with the Discovery Play of their first term. If they come to enjoy this style, they will ultimately find a freedom within the precise discipline demanded by it.

The projects of the third year should be performed in the school's theatre and be open to the whole school and invited guests, including members of the student's family. Press representatives and agents are not yet allowed to be present.

THE FOURTH YEAR—The Performing Year

With the beginning of the fourth year, the teaching aspect of the rehearsals is more or less finished. The emphasis is now on full production of plays with performances for public audiences, the press and agents. Public approval—or disapproval—and press criticism can teach a young actor a great deal about himself and the many hazards of his profession. He should be alert to such reactions and study the results they have had on him. But, during a performance, he must learn not to be thrown by any signs of disapproval from the audience.

The first play of this year should be a Shakespearian or Greek tragedy and it should be fully produced with sets, costumes and makeup. The two remaining terms should be given over to the preparation of a "Repertory Season" that should run in the school's theatre for two or three weeks. The programme of this season should be planned so that each student is seen in a variety of styles and in some sort of specially devised experimental piece that will reveal the range of his training and talent.

Besides the time spent on rehearsals, it would be useful, in the fourth year, to go back to improvisation work with or without masks; the student of the fourth year will now be much freer, much more daring and inventive in his work. More selective experiments on the transition from improvisation based on specific scenes to the interpretation of those scenes can be done. In this sort of improvisation, in which the actor invents within the given framework of a text, he is not directed by his teacher/director, but, because his teacher acts as a kind of mirror, the student can judge whether he has been able to translate into actual practice what he has discovered in his improvisation work. Experiencing the freedom his less closely supervised work gives him can be most liberating and exhilarating to the student.

This fourth year should also be given over to special work that it would have been unwise to do during the first three years of the training; this can be attempted at this point because the students by now will be aware of the pitfalls that these exercises present and be better able to avoid them. Here is some of the work I am thinking of: exercises for quickly building up a climax of anger, frenzy or any other strong emotion, even though one may not feel that emotion at the moment; exercises in speed for the sake of speed in speech, etc.

Besides these, there should be a series of short specialised courses of four to five weeks designed to acquaint the student with subjects which lie outside the normal curriculum: realising the actualities of life in the professional theatre, there should be exercises in preparing a role in a very short time, a week if necessary, and then going on to another role. There might be a course on musical comedy, including tap-dancing and techniques for putting over popular songs.

As one will have seen from the foregoing, the idea is that students learn acting through gradual experience, without being consciously aware that they are learning. In this way, the student's technical equipment will have had time to grow during the previous three years, and attain, in the fourth, a level which allows him to respond to the demands his directors and the plays will make.

The Teacher/Director

For many years now the director has been predominant in the professional theatre to such an extent that one can say that our theatrical era has been that of the director. This development began at the turn of this century, with Gordon Craig, Adolphe Appia, Jacques Copeau, Max Reinhardt and Stanislavski: these great men were reformers in every sense of the word and it was they who brought about this predominance of the director. During this time the director acquired almost complete control over the choice of the play, the style of presentation and the casting. It is because of this centralised control by the director that some of the finest actors of our time agreed to become part of true ensemble companies.

Thanks to these reformers who cleared the ground, we could start afresh: today the stage is free of the clutter of unnecessary scenery and we are spared costumes which are slavishly faithful to historical detail or to contemporary fashion without being dramatically convincing. From their work we have gained a sharper sense of style, a more alert sense of rhythm and a way of acting in which rhetoric and detailed versimilitude are proscribed. We have, in short, a much franker stage convention, one which reflects the nature of the play without overburdening it. Efforts have been made in every style to reach a deep human realism—a poetry of reality—quite distinct from muddy naturalism.

These developments have also brought about changes in audiences. The present-day public, curious and eager, likes to be enthralled, but it also seizes on the meaning of things: it wants contemporary works which have something to say about the life and destiny of modern man and classical works which, either by allusion or by contrast, have a bearing on the present day. The content of a play is now more important than any aesthetic attitude: matter triumphs over manner. When I directed Laurence Olivier in *Oedipus Rex* for the Old Vic Company I gave a curtain speech comparing the horrendous happenings of the play to the Second World War that had ended just a year earlier. But curiously enough, although the audience seemed to understand immediately what I was saying, I was severely attacked in the press for this speech.

Why, when you come to think of it, *do* Shakespeare's plays have such a tremendous attraction for today's audiences—particularly in Europe, where the atrocious events our generation has lived through and witnessed are still so vibrantly alive in our memory?

Today, the power of the director has shifted. In some countries he is still predominant while in others he has become a kind of inventor of plays; that is to say, taking an existing play, he uses it as a vehicle for presenting *his* ideas rather than the author's. In other countries, the director's power has shifted as his relationship with the actors has changed and new ways of working together have evolved. Often the actor is given more liberty during the rehearsal period and the designer has become a true collaborator with the director. The ensemble of actors of former days has now been expanded to become an ensemble of all who work on a production.

In such cases, the director is becoming more like the conductor of an orchestra than the Olympian god of yesteryear.

Although it is important to have an intellectual understanding of the differences between the classical theatre and that formed during the revolution we spoke of earlier, the way to bring this about is to *demonstrate*, not just to inform, to present precise living examples rather than generalised dead theories.

To do this, teacher/directors should take the students through a series of placing exercises which take into account various kinds of stage architecture and demonstrate the difference between staging on a theatre-in-the-round stage, on a thrust stage or on a proscenium stage; this is to show that the demands of each are entirely different.

Far too many professional directors and designers seem not to be aware of this. This is why a modern theatre school, even of modest means, must have a flexible, good-sized stage to allow for experiment.

For these exercises the teacher/director should evolve ground-plans for each different style. The ground-plan is the embryo of the decor, it has no aesthetic importance; it is solely a plan for action. It indicates the actor's general entrances, exits and moves in the principal acting areas and it shows what will happen up-stage, downstage, on the fore- or thrust-stage or at the sides; it suggests where a large acting area, or a smaller one, is needed. This distribution of space on the stage must obey the demands of the play and its style, and foresee the sweep of its action from scene to scene, from act to act.

As we can see from this, consideration must be given to style when evolving the ground-plans for the placing exercises. A ground-plan for staging Chekhov cannot be prepared in the same way as one for staging Shakespeare. In Shakespeare the acting space and the circulation of the actors in it has a special signifi-cance; the rapport of place and poetry is vital. What counts is the *text*—its lyricism, its poetry, its structure; these determine the *geography* of the production and the general, grand circulation of its action. Following these, changes of the moves can be made without disturbing the breath of life of the play by unnecessary scenic interruptions.

Fourth-year student Kevin Kline in the Juilliard Drama Division's production of Gorki's *The Lower Depths*, directed by Boris Tumarin. *(Photo: Diane Gorodnitzki.)*

Fourth-year student Patti LuPone in the Juilliard Drama Division's production of Sheridan's *The School for Scandal*, directed by Gerald Freedman. *(Photo: Richard Whitmeyer.)*

In Chekhov, the text is comparatively unimportant; it is a reflection of other things—psychological states, moods, the general atmosphere of the moment, the life given to objects—made significant by the way they are used.

In a realistic play, the moves of the actors, as well as their language, are more or less fragmented, as in life. But when one works on a play of a more formal style, where the shape of the language counts, it should be immediately evident that the circulation of the actors, the entire geography of the production, will reveal the style and meaning of the work in a visible and tangible manner.

I have often told my students that if the actors in a play could leave the imprint of their moves on the floor of the stage, one would be able to determine the genre of the play by reading the diagram left by these imprints. Plays by Congreve or Marivaux would leave curved, interlaced imprints; no doubt this would also happen with Molière. But in the case of the Greek, influenced primarily by the architecture of their theatres, such a diagram would be of extreme simplicity and purity in a clearly defined central space.

L'ENVOI

This book is the sum of fifty years experience in many countries. The principal conclusion I have come to is that one never stops learning.

If somebody asked my advice—which I never give—I would say: be open, be a learner—in the widest sense of the word—don't ever stop learning, however much training you may have. It is only when you go out into the profession that you will begin to discover how much more you have to learn and how hard you will have to fight to apply what you have learned already.

Acting is a balance between technique and inspiration; neither can do without the other.

Acting is like holding a bird in your hand—if you close your hand too tightly, the bird will be killed; if you open it too much, the bird will fly away.

PART TWO

THE PRODUCTION COURSE

In a way, it is the author who directs the director
to direct his play.

THE PRODUCTION COURSE attempts to prepare students for all
professional work on the stage with the exception of acting.

It is evident that a school which intends to form directors,
designers and theatre technicians must create a climate which
encourages the discussion of ideas; ideas about the world at large,
its civilization, the arts in general and all phases of theatre in
particular.

Certainly a director or a designer must have ideas. But these
ideas must be based on a knowledge of the stage and actors and
on a comprehension and appreciation of the playwright's work.

It is important, although difficult, to avoid unnecessary and
fruitless exchanges of ideas; we must try to prevent students from
losing their way in theoretical discussions, instead of following
the path of practical experience of the work.

It is easy to have too many ideas; it is also easy to try to extract
from an idea for staging a play an originality which, in fact, may
prove ineffectual if the idea itself is not a sound one. It is much
more difficult to discipline a fertile imagination, to force it to
question itself and to oblige it to submit to the masterpiece at
hand. But it is only by doing this that real originality comes into
play.

It is important to make every effort to instill in directors, designers and stage managers a sense of respect and responsibility
vis-à-vis a play and develop in them a cultivated and artistic sen-

sibility. This can be done as we train the students to be knowledgeable in stage techniques and able to deal with actors, backstage personnel and the specialists in the workshops.

My experience is that young people who want to become directors or stage designers have an inclination, at first, to intellectualise theatre. This is understandable since most of them have prepared themselves through academic courses and cultural studies, apprenticeships in university or college theatres, or by frequenting lunchtime theatres in London or off-off Broadway workshops in New York.

But their understanding of the *actor's* metier is often vague, because they usually have not gone through the experience of acting and do not understand what goes on inside an actor. They do not know what the actor has to do to build up a character in a play from moment to moment; they have no conception of the different phases the actor goes through in order to lift the text of the play from the printed page and make it come to life in performance before an audience.

The work in this Production Course should be organised in such a way that all elements are examined in the right order and at the right time.

The course is divided into three parts which cover three years. The first year is called Production Course A, the second, Production Course B, and the third, the Advanced Course. At the end of the first two years, the student's work is evaluated to determine whether it is advisable for him to continue.

In order to enter the course, the student must have some background in world civilization, literature (especially dramatic literature), art history and music. Design students must also have some practical experience in drawing and painting. Once in the programme, they will have little time to acquire basic, essential cultural and artistic tools. The function of a drama school is to help the student to orient such acquired knowledge to the theatre.

Although the courses are basically designed to produce directors, designers and theatre technicians, all students in this course have to be trained in the elementary techniques of the stage before concentrating on their own special vocations.

It will be possible at the end of the first year to see, more or less clearly, for which work the student is particularly well suited.

Or the student himself may discover gradually that another branch appeals to him more than the one which originally attracted him.

It has often been said that it is not possible to train directors; this is true only if a student intending to become a director enters the Production Course expecting that he will learn directing by immediately being put to the task. This does not happen until the student has gone through the first year of the preliminary training and is accepted for the Central Class in the second year of the Production Course.

Production Course A

This is the basic course, covering the elementary techniques of the stage. All students, whatever their specialisation, must become thoroughly acquainted with the technical aspects of the stage. Here is a rough enumeration of some of them:

1) The stage and its equipment. This covers types of stages, floors, ceilings, what is underneath a stage, etc.
2) Scenery. Talks and demonstrations by the master carpenter on various methods of building scenery, on the evolution of scenery construction—new materials, new techniques, etc. The students go on to actual practice in building scenery, flats, doors, ceilings and windows. They also learn how to prepare gauzes and scrims; how to plan packs of scenery for touring.
3) Painting of scenery. First, there should be an explanation of the materials to be employed; the scene painter teaching the course should talk about the different kinds of paint which are used and the impact colour can have on an audience. He should also touch upon the way colours change under artificial lighting.

   The next step is for the students to practice scene painting. They are taught first the rudiments of the techniques before going on to copy designs from sketches onto canvas. They are given small pieces of canvas which they have to prepare; then they mix different kinds of colours and paint a simple design onto the canvas—a tree or such like. They are also taught how to suggest stone or wood through painting. It is only later, when the work in the Design Course develops, that they will learn how to paint perspectives or trompe l'oeil; how to copy from scene-designs and enlarge them on a canvas.

4) Properties. The teacher will explain what constitutes a prop, how a set is dressed, how hand props, snow, stage meals and drinks are made. He will also show the students how to construct stage models and make masks.

5) Lighting. Talks on the history of lighting the stage should be given by a master electrician. What is light? What are the basic principles of electricity, what is the function of the various pieces of stage-lighting apparatus? How does one mix colours? How does one run a switchboard? All this should be covered in lectures and demonstrations; then there must be practice with actual equipment. The directors and designers will later study these elements from the artistic point of view as they are related to specific plays.

6) Terminology of the stage. This the students learn as they go along in their practical work.

7) Ground-plans, also called floor plans. This part of the training is particularly important for directors and designers. The ground-plan is the embryo of the production of a play and the ability to prepare one is one of the basic tools of staging. From the ground-plan the director determines the moves of his actors and from it the designer makes the elevation for his set designs. In learning how to prepare ground-plans, the student will learn how to make precise measurements, how to draw to scale, and so on. Later on, he will be given existing ground-plans to copy and will be shown the reasons why they vary from play to play. The next stage is in the domain of interpretation: the student will be given one act of a play and asked to draw a workable ground-plan, based on his understanding of the necessities of the play in question. The practice of drawing ground-plans for different kinds of plays and for different styles will go on, with ever-increasing demands on the student, for the whole three years of the training.

Even though student/directors will not actually have to build or paint scenery, it is useful for them to be present at the classes where that is taught in order to learn about the main principles of scene construction and painting and also to learn about the terminology. Then they will later be able to tell a carpenter or scene painter clearly what they require. Of course, the student/designer will have to learn how to paint scenery.

By the middle of their first year the student/directors should begin to comprehend something of the experience of acting. To assure this, they are taken, under the guidance of one of the teacher/directors, to watch classes in the Acting Course. They should observe the work in the movement classes, in the improvisation classes and, later, watch rehearsals.

Running concurrently with these courses, there is one we call Imaginative Background (see Chapter Five). The Imaginative Background talks and lectures are attended by students from both the Acting and Production Courses; in fact, the pictorial documentation used in that work is prepared by students in the Production Course; they do the research on periods and gather material for the exhibits, such as photographs, costumes, props, pictures, furniture, etc.

The main aim of this section of the Production Course is to teach the students how to do research, what to look for in preparing a reference portfolio documenting styles of different periods. By the end of his studies, each student/director and designer should have his own complete collection of such material.

In their first year the student/designers learn how to construct to scale a model stage, perhaps even several of them, which they will use throughout their years of study for trying out their set designs.

Toward the end of the first year, we begin to deal with the processes of preparing the production of a play. In collaboration, a student/director and a student/designer learn how to plan a production, how to budget a show, how to make lighting, music and special-effect plots.

During the course of this work the students will be told about box-office duties and front-of-house management. Several talks should be given on such administrative matters as preparing contracts, dealing with unions, and managing touring companies.

These introductory courses must not pretend to do more than give elementary knowledge of the techniques. Even in the first year of these elementary courses it should be made clear that the techniques are there to nourish and serve dramatic invention, never to dominate it.

Students who have fulfilled the requirements of the first year can stay on to continue their training in the second. But, nevertheless, if for some reason, a student is obliged to leave the school at the end of only one year, this training will qualify him for a job as assistant stage manager or as assistant to one or another of the other stage technicians. In this way he will be able to find a place for himself in the theatre.

Production Course B

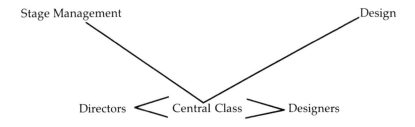

STAGE MANAGEMENT

This course develops the training further. In the beginning it includes both student directors and designers, but the designers drop out after a while as they have their own specialised courses.

The Stage Management Course deals with both theory and practice. At the outset, the teacher describes the duties and responsibilities of each member of the staff both during rehearsals and during the run of the show.

The stage staff includes, among others, such people as the production manager, the master carpenter and electrician, the wardrobe mistress, the callboy and the stage-door keeper. Among his other duties, the stage manager has to know about salary scales, about departmental accounts and how they are processed for payment. He also must know such things as where to find the nearest doctor!

The student must become familiar with the many rules and regulations governing theatre buildings, particularly the fire regulations.

The qualities a good stage manager must have are diverse; his long training must be both technical *and* human. Above all he needs to have great self-discipline and strong nerves—anything may happen in the theatre and *he* will be held responsible, whether he is or not.

We want our students to become competent artist-technicians with a responsible attitude towards their work, capable of exercising their practical *and* artistic knowledge while running a show; we want them to become professionals, who can command respect from workmen and artists alike.

All the students in this course will eventually serve as stage managers for the shows given in the Acting programme. In the beginning they will only be required to prepare the rehearsal rooms or the stage, by marking the floor with tape to indicate the ground-plan and setting the stage with rehearsal sets and rehearsal furniture. They will be responsible for seeing to it that the cast are all present and on stage in good time. They will have to see to it that the rehearsal room or stage is cleared after each rehearsal and left ready for the next.

During rehearsals they will write down in a prompt-book all the production notes and the staging given to the actors by the director. This, the stage manager's prompt-book, is like a nerve-center on which everything connected with a production converges. Later they will also be shown how to prepare scripts for the actors. A stage manager must also learn how to rehearse the cast if necessary and deal with all understudy rehearsals.

SPECIAL EFFECTS

During their second year the students in this course will learn how to produce special effects, such as wind, rain, thunder and lightning. There should be practical demonstrations of existing machines, but experimentation to improve on these—or perhaps even to find new ways of producing effects—should be encouraged. The student designers too might try their hand at inventing special-effects devices.

At the end of this work, the students should be assigned scenes from plays and asked to work out effect plots for them. When they have done that and are ready to demonstrate them, other students should be asked by the teacher to read the texts, so that the effects can be tried out on cue.

LIGHTING

As the students continue their theoretical and practical work on lighting, they will learn more about mixing colours, focussing, dimmers, spotlights, cyclorama lighting and wiring. There should also be a whole section on projection of painted scenery. Finally, the students plan the lighting for an entire play, with a complete lighting plot and cues. This culminates in a practical demonstration of their skill at the switchboard.

MAKE-UP AND WIGS

Student/directors and designers will together go through a course dealing with stage make-up, wigs, beards and moustaches.

They should be taught the rudiments of colour mixing and blending, how to shape a face, how to indicate shadows and lines, how to make up eyes and mouths, etc. After first using their own faces, they should then practice on one another.

Let them study faces in famous paintings and try to copy them on their own. Rembrandt, Breughel, Goya, El Greco, Watteau, George Grosz and Modigliani are especially useful for this. They should first copy these faces in simple lines on paper and then try to create a make-up design from that. Following their design they first apply make-up to their own or to a fellow student's face. Ultimately they must be able to show an actor how to do this himself.

STAGE DESIGN

Nowadays, due to changes in theatre architecture, the position of the stage designer is in transition. Faced with many exciting challenges, the stage designer oscillates constantly between being an artist-designer-painter and being a gifted theatre technician.

What qualities should we look for in selecting students for this course? Talent as a creative painter or architect? Technical ability as a man of the theatre?

The ideal student is one who is, before anything else, an artist —an artist who has a feeling for form, who can draw and who has a rich and sensitive palette. With us he will learn how to use more fully his sense of proportion, his appreciation for different materials and, finally, his feeling for the extraordinary emotional value of colour and light. He should have something of the architect in him, but he must be a person who is willing to submit to the laws of the stage; he must design what can be constructed, he must find ways to give full scope to the dramatic action of a play while permitting the complete unfolding of its style.

It is through constant exposure to great authors, through continual reading and studying of plays, that the student designers are gradually transformed into true artists of the theatre, people who are devoted to the task of translating to the stage, in concrete terms, the meaning and the spirit of a play.

It is likely that our student/designers will come from art schools, where they will already have had training in drawing, painting, sculpture and, perhaps, architecture. We will show them how to put their talents as painters, architects or sculptors at the disposal of the theatre.

Here are a few guiding principles for the student/designer:

- Although his designs should have an artistic and interpretative quality, because he is responsible for the construction and painting of sets made from them, the designer's working drawings must be precise, with detailed measurements that will enable the workshops to execute his intentions correctly. The same applies to costume designs.
- The student designer *must* have an aptitude for drawing, so that he can communicate his scenic conception to his collaborators.

The designer's contribution to a play goes far beyond that of an artist or draftsman. The shapes and colours of his sets and costumes are not meant to remain flat on paper; they must live in three-dimensional space. His designs must be interpreted and accentuated according to a *perspective of theatre,* a perspective in which the primary element is the perception of these sets and costumes by an audience. For example, a costume cannot simply be visualized as a painted image on paper or even thought of in the same way as a tailor conceives of everyday clothes for a client. Too often designers disguise an actor instead of dressing a character in a play. Or they imprison the actor in a costume which is historically accurate or decorative, but has very little dramatic value.

A costume can either aid or hinder an actor in meeting the special demands of a character. A costume is in itself a kind of construction. I call it a "kind of construction" because it is built around an actor's physique, a physique which frequently has to be modified.

This fact—that a costume cannot be simply a painted image on paper—is often very difficult to convey to a student/designer. The design *must* be alive and dramatic on paper, but it must also be easy for the cutters and seamstresses in the workshops to "read." It is useful to begin by asking the student to make small figurines of wire and straw about ten to twelve inches high. Then assign him a character from a play which he already knows and ask him to dress one of the figurines, in character, with bits and pieces of real material. When this has been done, ask him to sketch the figurine he has just dressed and try to make the sketch as alive as the figurine existing in three dimensional space. To go further, have him make other sketches of his own invention and try, from these, to dress the figurines. This two-way practice will, in the end, be very helpful to him.

The colours, as well as the shapes, of costumes and sets must always be viewed from that perspective of theatre I talked about earlier. The artificial light of the stage will alter colours as they are perceived in scenic space. This must be considered before the costumes and sets leave the workshops. It is also essential that the designer take into consideration the alterations, the transformations, that take place because of the special optics of the theatre.

I have always encouraged my design students to carry a sketchbook about with them and sketch whenever they can. They should do quick sketches during rehearsals, attempting to catch characteristic moves, positions and expressions. They should sketch faces of people and movements of animals—anything that catches their eye and develops their faculties of observation.

CARPENTRY

Designers, first of all, deal with the technical aspects of design: they must know how to draw a piece of scenery to exact measurements, how to indicate the dimensions of furniture and other props, how to show clearly on the design the way pieces of scenery are put together and how they are held up.

Perspective drawing is involved in preparing the elevation—the next step in going from the ground-plan to the execution of the design.

For this, the student should be given perspective designs to copy, with special reference to the masters of the Italian School—such as Piranesi.

PAINTING

In the scene-painting course the students will learn how to paint backcloths and stage carpets; how to paint architectural views; how to prepare transparencies; they will learn methods to use in painting marble, wood, mirrors. They will learn how to dye canvas and other materials for decor and costumes and, when necessary, how to paint directly on those materials.

Having learned the rudiments of painting on canvas in their first year, the students will now be shown how to interpret the colours of a design and how to transfer a design onto small canvasses in frames. Finally the master-teacher will demonstrate how to paint on large surfaces and then let the students themselves try it.

At the end of their second year the students will, under the guidance of their teachers, design, build and paint the backcloths and sets for the third-year students' shows.

Before going on to costume design and making, I want to say a few general words on colour.

COLOUR

In the theatre, it is vital to study the emotional value of colour. The relationship between the spoken text the ear hears and the form and colours the eye sees produces an emotion that is difficult to explain or analyse, an emotion which, therefore, cannot easily be consciously produced.

Although many of our students will have graduated from art schools and, supposedly, will have done some painting, they generally have very little notion of the wide variety of colours that exist. Red, for them, is red and yellow is yellow; that is all.

The student will have to become aware of the subtle balances involved in the relationships between tone and colour. By practical experiments he will come to recognise the whole gamut of tones that one colour can have: all the blues, all the reds, all the yellows, etc. An exercise that is useful in showing the relationship between a colour and its different tones—while at the same time teaching the limitations imposed by the special optics of the stage—is to try out various tones of colours in frames of different shapes: round ones, square ones, oval ones, etc. By doing this, the student will develop, among other things, an awareness of how certain tones predominate over others and how these colour-shapes seem to alter as they are placed in various juxtapositions.

Costume Design

The first, the basic, principle to make the student aware of in teaching costume design is that costumes for the stage, although based on everyday clothes that people wear, must have a scenic, a dramatic character. In short, the student must discover the difference between a dress worn in real life and the same kind of dress worn in a play on a stage. It is only when the student has become aware of this difference that the question of how to deal with the interpretation of a character in a play through his costumes, or how, indeed, to deal with the question of the style of the play, can be resolved.

While he is working on this, the student is also sketching from live models: first in pencil, then in pen and ink. After a while the student begins to draw, not with pencil or pen, but exclusively with a brush, using only colour to give form; he may not use a pencil to indicate shape. In preparing a design, he should arrive at the colour by "drawing" with colour, so that it becomes a living, essential element of the design and not just something added to it.

COSTUME MAKING

There is a very real difference between making a costume and making a dress or a suit. What seems right on the street is often not right on the stage; what is acceptable when seen nearby may not be so when seen from far away. Many fabrics, colours and textures, although they may seem identical to those indicated on the design, will be quite different when affected by stage lighting.

Since costumes must be cleaned and ironed frequently, any kind of decoration must be firmly sewn on. It is also more important to have strong seams than a fine finish on the inside of the costume. The costume must be practical—quick to get into *and* out of: the fasteners must be easy to work.

In practice, the student first learns how to cut patterns in paper, then in muslin. Only then does he learn the various ways of cutting the chosen material. He practices with certain basic elements: bodices and sleeves—in one piece and in two—shirts and trousers, etc.

After this, the student practices, first, sewing by hand, then on a machine. He will have to learn how to take measurements and how to do fittings. It is only after mastering these practical skills that he will begin to work on the individual problems that arise when cutting and making period costumes.

It is usually best to start with the 19th century and then go on to the more complicated styles of previous ones.

At the end of their second year the design students should be asked to participate in the planning, designing and actual making of the costumes for the acting students' annual performances.

THE CENTRAL CLASS

To be chosen for the Central Class for directors and designers should be the inspiration for all students in the Production Course B, where indeed the work is subtly directed towards what will be done in this Central Class. It is not a technical class, but is devoted to the study, as in the Acting Course, of plays in the three principal categories we have mentioned before.

Although in their first year the students will have been made aware of differences in style, because of time limitations, this awareness was only developed in a very summary way. In the Central Class the student will be able to go further in his researches.

The student directors and designers will study the three plays—one play per term—under the guidance of a teacher/director and will prepare a production from its conception to the beginning of the rehearsals; it is now that they will first be confronted with the pleasures and problems of collaboration in the production of a play.

In the Central Class we attempt to lead the students to an appreciation of the essential nature of each play and, by doing so, enable them to clarify their own basic attitude towards it. In order to do this, we stress the importance of the way in which they first read a play: that they must be open to the initial, immediate impact of the play's specific character, i.e. *what* it is saying and *how* it is said. But to understand the *how* requires a deeper study of the text and its meaning. During the first reading, the impact of the play may be primarily on the reader's feelings. But there may be intellectual excitement at the same moment that the student's first ideas about rhythm, colour and tempo are being born. Such initial impressions are most precious, but one must not adopt them irrevocably at once. One must not throw oneself on a first idea; certainly one must not decide about a definite form for staging a play until the "meaning"—in French, "le sens"—of the play has revealed itself. It is only through continuous reading and re-reading of the play, in a semi-detached way, that one can come to some tentative conclusions.

It takes time to become aware of a text's composition, its rhythm and colour, its general mood. It is only gradually that a play begins to live inside one. The work of the director is, after all, to translate into form and action, into characters and sound, that which lies dormant in the text. In a way, it is the author who directs the director to direct his play.

In the first phase of the Central Class, it is very important, and sometimes very difficult, to make the student/director understand quite clearly that he will not be given formulas and shortcuts which will enable him to reduce his production schemes to a few simple procedures that will achieve something real and valid.

The Advanced Course

At the end of the second year a small number of exceptionally talented students from the Director's and Designer's Course are chosen for a further year of intense study of play production. This selection is based on the individual student's artistic achievements.

This course is both a forum for discussion and a place for research and experiment but it is at the same time a place where the student can obtain a solid grounding in the more conventional techniques of the stage. It is vital to show the student that theatrical conventions are constantly being questioned and that he himself will be a participant in their evolution. Therefore, we must encourage him to plunge into his work in a spirit of inquisitiveness.

The work in the Advanced Course proceeds in a way similar to that of the Central Class.

Students again work in the three basic categories of plays but now each student director works with a different designer on each play in the three different styles.

Until this time the student directors have not yet worked with actors, and their first study of how to rehearse, for the initial play at least, will be more or less theoretical. When I taught this class we discussed the kind of acting the chosen play needed and compared it to the acting appropriate to other styles. From time to time I would use the student directors and designers to demonstrate relevant points. We would also discuss the different phases of rehearsals and how the director's treatment of the actor changes from one phase to another.

To illustrate these theoretical discussions, we devised placing exercises using short scenes from the play in hand. These exercises were at first done with other students in the Advanced Course, but later in the year we used any acting students who might be free. In this way, each of the directors would do exercises in all three categories of plays. The same placing exercises done in a theatre-in-the-round, on a thrust stage or on a proscenium stage will also show that the demands of each are entirely different. In today's theatre, it is essential to realise this.

In the last part of the year we did a complete production of a play with the acting students.

In addition, the student/directors are asked to watch rehearsals of the third- and fourth-year acting students and serve as assistants to the teacher/directors. The designers, while collaborating with their fellow student/directors on their own productions, also serve as assistants to the professional designers working on the shows given by the graduating acting students.

Besides this work, there are also more detailed lectures and informal talks on the History of Theatre and the Arts. The students are also encouraged to read as many plays of different styles as possible, and to read poetry aloud, either by themselves or to each other.

Before concluding this section, I would like to add a final word about designers and directors.

DESIGNERS

Designers, in the past, have usually been much too specialised. To the detriment of the play's fundamental dramatic life, they were either artists with little stage technique or technicians with limited artistry.

Today the role of the designer in the theatre also reflects recent changes in theatre architecture. As I see it, a designer should be able to deal with set *and* costume designs of both the modern and the classical repertory. But whether he does sets or costumes, or both, he will have to work differently for the Greek or Elizabethan stage, the proscenium stage, the theatre in the round or the thrust stage. He has become an essential collaborator and not merely a technician at the director's disposal. It is he who must ultimately give colour and shape to the author's and director's vision and, consequently, to the actor's.

The designer is placed between the director, on the one hand, and the technicians responsible for executing the work, on the other. In his role as *inventor* he must grasp the essence of the play and understand clearly the director's concept of it. This will enable him to provide the director with a variety of creative designs for the production from which the director can choose. In his role as *executor* he must have competence and authority and always be in control of the technical side of the work.

With well-run workshops today it is possible for the designer to delegate the preparation of working drawings, elevations and so forth to assistants. This, of course, gives the contemporary designer more time to devote to the creative problems the rapid evolution of theatre architecture has presented him with. The designer is no longer someone who just "decorates the stage;" he now makes an essential contribution to the life of the production on a par with its author and director.

The relationship between a director and his designer is a very delicate one: much depends on their personalities and their willingness to give and take.

Once a director develops a concept in accord with the style of the play he wants to do, he must evolve a ground-plan. If he hesitates or is slow in deciding upon his staging, he may find that the designer has proceeded independently and he may, therefore, be limited to the plan the designer has devised. On the other hand, a director who is too rigid in imposing his ideas might find that true collaboration is difficult.

DIRECTORS

It is often difficult for a student/director to hold back his understandable desire to see his production on its feet, difficult for him to be patient with himself and with his actors.

As he will have read the play he wants to direct many times, he will already have a vision of it. But, at the first reading with his actors, he may be surprised by what he *hears*, which may in no way be consistent with his own first concept. This is quite normal and he should not worry too much. A director has to learn how to *hear* and how to *see*; he has to know how to keep himself outside the play, how to listen to it as the actors speak, how to watch it when, later, the actual rehearsals begin. He will slowly come to ideas of form; he will hear the timbre and the volume of voice the characters need; he will find the general—and the particular—pace of the play. He must stay outside the play until what he hears and sees gradually merges with his own vision.

He should enter the play gradually, avoiding preconceived ideas. Accepting the confusion that at first exists, he should proceed cooly, not attempting to precipitate anything, but allowing the play slowly to unfold.

As for style, it seems to me that whatever political or social opinion a director has, whatever his aesthetic tendencies, what he does in the theatre must be based on a comprehension of and a respect for style.

I am the first to acknowledge that theatre must be interpreted from a contemporary point of view, whether one uses Greek plays like *Oedipus Rex* or Italian plays like Goldoni's *The Servant of Two Masters*.

We have to re-invent the past, *but* with a proper regard for it. Only then will we achieve style and actuality. We must understand that the reality, the style, of a play is as important as the reality of a grocer or a newsvendor. Works of art speak a direct language that is beyond reason. In the same way that it would be unthinkable to alter the Parthenon, a statue or a painting, a dramatic work, too, has a style with such power of expression that it should be an article of faith of all true men of the theatre that this style must be preserved at all costs.

INDEX OF NAMES

INDEX OF CHAPTERS
THREE-SEVEN

MICHEL SAINT-DENIS

When Michel Saint-Denis' first book, *Theatre: The Rediscovery of Style*, was published, after observing that "this book ranks with Stanislavski's *My Life in Art*," *Library Journal* called Saint-Denis "the greatest theorist of the theatre alive today." As Sir Peter Hall has written, "four major theatres—the Royal Court, the National Theatre, the English National Opera and the Royal Shakespeare Company—owe part of their way of working to him." The London Theatre Studio, the Royal Shakespeare Company Studio, the Old Vic Theatre Centre, the Centre National de l'Est in France and the National Theatre School of Canada, as well as the Drama Division of the Juilliard School in New York, were all based on his way of training. John Houseman found that "without question, Saint-Denis was the acknowledged leader and innovator in the field of professional theatre training." "It was an education and a delight to watch Michel's rehearsals. His brilliant talents entitled him to the devotion he inspired in all those who had the good fortune to work with him," said Sir John Gielgud. Remarking on the "peculiar spellbinding quality of Saint-Denis' teaching," Lord Olivier has written, "Saint-Denis had a clairvoyant divination into the soul of acting . . . . I was entirely happy and confident in blindly accepting even his minutest direction without question. . . . His production of *Oedipus* was a brilliant success and so—thanks entirely to him, in my considered opinion—was my performance." Harold Clurman found him "the most cultivated, innately refined, spiritually pure person I have ever encountered in the theatre." For Sir Michael Redgrave, Michel Saint-Denis was "a great director, a great artist, a great man." Jerzy Grotowski called him "my spiritual father." "Working with Michel Saint-Denis opened up a new world for me," remembered Sir Colin Davis, "I carry that experience with me always, seeking the same dedication to dramatic truth he taught me gave the theatre its proper dignity." Sir Alec Guinness wrote, "his influence on all of us has been tremendous. . . . For my own part, my debt to him is quite colossal. . . . He really illumined acting for me."

SURIA SAINT-DENIS

After studying theatre arts, music, drama and dance in Paris, Berlin, Milan and London, Suria Saint-Denis toured Europe with her own company, for which she wrote and directed a number of experimental stage productions combining speech, chant, mime and dance. She served as Assistant to her husband, Michel Saint-Denis, both at his London Theatre Studio and at the Old Vic Theatre Centre and School and during the Second World War she started a nationwide movement for theatre for young people, which later became the Young Vic Company. She was Director of the theatre school attached to the Centre Dramatique de l'Est in France and set up the curriculum of the National Theatre School of Canada, of whose Board of Governors she is a Life Member. Madame Saint-Denis was Assistant to Sir John Gielgud for his productions of *The Beggar's Opera* and *Macbeth*, to David Lean for his film *Great Expectations* with Sir Alec Guinness and to G. Pascal for his celebrated film version of Shaw's *Caesar and Cleopatra* starring Vivien Leigh and Claude Rains. She has coached singers in acting and mime at the Paris Opera and, in 1981, she acted as Consultant for Mask Work at the Metropolitan Opera in New York, coaching singers for John Dexter's production of Stravinsky's *Oedipus Rex*. She set up the curriculum for the Drama Division of the Juilliard School where she has been the Assistant Director of The Drama Division since 1967 and Consultant Director since 1971.